A NATION
AT THE
CROSSROADS

SPIRITUAL DECLINE
IN THE
PROMISED LAND

A NATION AT THE CROSSROADS

SPIRITUAL DECLINE IN THE PROMISED LAND

Revised and Expanded Edition of
Choosing the Fulness

S. Michael Wilcox

BOOKCRAFT
Salt Lake City, Utah

Library of Congress Catalog Card Number: 99-72287

ISBN 1-57008-628-1

First Printing, 1999

Printed in the United States of America

Wherefore, men are free according to the flesh; and all things are given them which are expedient unto man. And they are free to choose liberty and eternal life, through the great Mediator of all men, or to choose captivity and death, according to the captivity and power of the devil.

—2 Nephi 2:27

CONTENTS

INTRODUCTION

O<small>NE OF THE MOST BEAUTIFUL</small> chapters in all scripture is the seventh chapter of Moses in the Pearl of Great Price. It contains a vision recorded by Enoch that covers all time and describes the two roads mankind may walk: the road that leads to Zion, exaltation, and oneness with the Godhead, or the road that leads to Babylon, destruction, and captivity with the adversary.

In this remarkable vision Enoch is shown the joy, peace, and happiness of Zion, but he is also led by the Lord to understand and have compassion for "the residue" who face destruction. "Zion have I blessed," the Lord states, "but the residue of the people have I cursed" (Moses 7:20). The vision repeatedly shifts from pole to pole. Enoch beholds that "Zion, in process of time, was taken up into heaven . . . even in the bosom of the Father, and of the Son" (Moses 7:21, 24). Immediately thereafter he beholds that "the power of Satan was upon all the face of the earth" (Moses 7:24). "Generation upon generation" passes by his eyes, and he sees the "misery" and "wickedness" of man (Moses 7:41).

At the height of the vision Enoch sees two fathers' faces. The first face is that of the "father of all lies" (Moses 4:4), the second that of God. Further contemplating the generations of the earth, Enoch beholds "Satan; and he had a great chain in his hand, and it veiled the whole face of the earth with darkness; and he looked up and laughed, and his angels rejoiced" (Moses 7:26).

In contrast to this exultant, mocking face, Enoch beholds the face of God. He describes that vision in beautiful terms: "How is it that the heavens weep, and shed forth their tears as the rain upon the mountains?" (Moses 7:28.)

All mankind must choose which face they desire to serve

and which road they will walk. Both roads end in a fulness, either the fulness of iniquity or the fulness of light and truth. The scriptures plainly testify of the attitudes, actions, thoughts, and desires that lead to either fulness. As Enoch saw, the choice would be presented to all generations.

In the last days the roads are clearly marked. The world is rapidly following the "residue" of Enoch's time, while the Church is diligently seeking to establish Zion. The distance between them broadens with every passing year. This puts a great responsibility upon the Saints. They must leave the world, gather the elect, and build a Zion society.

This book focuses on the two fulnesses toward which mankind in the "dispensation of the fulness of times" is heading. With the help of the scriptures the evils that constitute a fulness of iniquity will be described and contrasted with the characteristics of a Zion people. The scriptural record will allow us to draw plain and easily recognized comparisons between ancient societies, both good and bad, and the modern world, and will also allow us to examine closely the Lord's counsels to the Saints. In light of these great opposites it is critical for us as members of the Lord's kingdom in the last days to understand how to obtain a fulness of light, truth, and intelligence, as it is taught by the Lord and his prophets.

Both fulnesses are plainly described in the scriptures, especially in the Book of Mormon. It is, perhaps, the best source for understanding the roads men choose to walk, with their inevitable consequences. A comprehension of both roads will help every man, woman, and child choose with intelligence the fulness he or she desires to obtain. In the end all will see the face toward which they have been progressing. May there be many who choose the fulness offered by the Father who wept for the residue, shedding forth his tears as rain upon the mountains.

1

A Fulness of Joy

WHEN I ENTERED THE MISSION field as a new missionary, my zone leader took me tracting one afternoon to teach me "the proper method," as he called it. He stood with his toes to the door, set his face with determination and soberness, then declared in a tone of warning that we were messengers of Jesus Christ. This usually brought one of two reactions: either a deep look of puzzlement that such seriousness could come from such a nice-looking boy, or else fright, which resulted in a quick closing of the door. When I was asked to present the gospel in like manner, I balked. There was no spirit in the approach, no joy, no invitation to hear the "glad news" of Christ's atonement and the Restoration. Though my earnest and well-meaning mentor didn't know it, his manner suggested that the gospel did not fill him with joy.

Several months later I too was asked to train a new missionary, Elder N__. I will never forget him. He was less than five feet tall and almost as wide. His French was broken, spoken with a Utah accent, and very difficult to understand. He was a little absent-minded. (I remember watching him crack six eggs and drop them one by one into the burner instead of the pan, and then later wash the dishes with cooking oil instead of detergent.) He didn't have any sense of direction. He got trapped for two minutes in an elevator because he didn't realize the door to enter on the first floor was not the same as the exit door on the second floor. He was found wanting to some degree in virtually every aspect of missionary work—

except one. He absolutely radiated joy. He was thrilled to be serving the Lord. He was in love with the gospel and had taken its messages to heart, and happiness shone from his eyes and his smile. He was a living invitation to drink from the well of life. From Elder N__ I learned a great deal about the effects of the gospel.

Joseph Smith once wrote:

> Happiness is the object and design of our existence; and will be the end thereof, if we pursue the path that leads to it; and this path is virtue, uprightness, faithfulness, holiness, and keeping all the commandments of God. But we cannot keep all the commandments without first knowing them, and we cannot expect to know all, or more than we now know unless we comply with or keep those we have already received. (*Teachings of the Prophet Joseph Smith,* sel. Joseph Fielding Smith [Salt Lake City: Deseret Book Co., 1938], pp. 255–56.)

It is clear that God wishes his children to be happy and to eventually receive a "fulness of joy" in his "presence," where there are "pleasures for evermore" (Psalm 16:11). The Prophet Joseph Smith has outlined the path that leads to that fulness.

Among the many commandments given in scripture, there is one we often overlook. It is usually given by way of comfort or encouragement, but it is a commandment just the same. The Lord constantly reminds his children to be joyful, happy, and of good cheer, to rejoice and to lift up their heads. At least forty sections of the Doctrine and Covenants contain exhortations of this kind. The Lord often issues this encouragement in the most distressing or discouraging of circumstances. To express joy is an act of gratitude which shows the Father that we acknowledge and appreciate the multitude of blessings he has given us. This Nephi plainly taught in 2 Nephi 4:

> O then, if I have seen so great things, if the Lord in his condescension unto the children of men hath visited men in so much mercy, why should my heart weep and my soul

linger in the valley of sorrow, and my flesh waste away, and my strength slacken, because of mine afflictions? . . .

Rejoice, O my heart, and cry unto the Lord, and say: O Lord, I will praise thee forever; yea, my soul will rejoice in thee, my God, and the rock of my salvation. (2 Nephi 4:26, 30.)

God desires his children to be righteous, because righteousness is synonymous with happiness. This truth Joseph Smith plainly taught, as we have seen. Lehi also taught his son Jacob this principle: "If there be no righteousness there be no happiness" (2 Nephi 2:13). He also told his son that "men are, that they might have joy" (2 Nephi 2:25). Joy as the object of existence is a prevalent message of the Book of Mormon and indeed of all scripture.

Mankind receives joy through righteousness and through the atonement of Jesus Christ. Without that atonement, Jacob testified, "we become devils, angels to a devil, to be shut out from the presence of our God, and to remain with the father of lies, in misery, like unto himself" (2 Nephi 9:9). Just prior to entering the Garden of Gethsemane Jesus told his "troubled" Apostles, "Be of good cheer; I have overcome the world" (John 16:33). His triumph over death and Satan allows all of humanity the opportunity to receive a "fulness of joy" at his "right hand" (Psalm 16:11). The Apostle Paul, contemplating the power of the Atonement, wrote to the Ephesian Saints of "the unsearchable riches of Christ" (Ephesians 3:8). In his epistle he includes a prayer "that Christ may dwell in your hearts by faith; that ye, being rooted and grounded in love, may be able to comprehend with all saints what is the breadth, and length, and depth, and height; and to know the love of Christ, which passeth knowledge, that ye might be filled with all the fulness of God" (Ephesians 3:17-19).

Early in the Book of Mormon we are presented with an image that sets the tone of all that follows. After traveling in his dream "for the space of many hours in darkness," Lehi relates, "I beheld a tree, whose fruit was desirable to make one happy. And it came to pass that I did go forth and partake of the fruit thereof; and I beheld that it was most sweet, above all that I ever before tasted. . . . And as I partook of the fruit thereof it filled my soul with exceedingly great joy." (1 Nephi 8:8–12.) Later, Nephi also sees the tree of his father's dream. After seeing the newborn Son of God in his mother's arms, Nephi is asked by an angel, "Knowest thou the meaning of the tree which thy father saw? And I answered him, saying: Yea, it is the love of God, which sheddeth itself abroad in the hearts of the children of men; wherefore, it is the most desirable above all things. And he spake unto me, saying: Yea, and the most joyous to the soul." (1 Nephi 11:21–23.) The invitation is extended to us all to partake of the fruit of the tree in order to be filled with joy.

To partake of the fruit of the tree of life should be the main desire of all Latter-day Saints. Our countenances, like that of Elder N___, should radiate the joy that living the gospel and receiving the Savior produces. When we consider all the blessings of the Atonement and the Restoration, are there any other people on the face of the earth who have more reason than we have to rejoice and to "sing the song of redeeming love" (Alma 5:26)? In a world of increasing despair, the Latter-day Saints truly have a message which proclaims "the good news."

In his great intercessory prayer, offered just before his agony in Gethsemane, Jesus prayed that his disciples "might have my joy fulfilled in themselves" (John 17:13). "I pray not that thou shouldest take them out of the world," he continued, "but that thou shouldest keep them from the evil" (John 17:15). In order to keep them from "evil" and to fill them with joy, he was willing to suffer the pains of his atonement. There was no price he was unwilling to pay to bring joy to his disciples. At the Last Supper he asked them, and those of future generations who would be his disciples, also to be willing to sacrifice in order to bring happiness and joy to themselves and to others.

The joy that Christ brings is an enduring happiness. The fruit of the tree can satisfy all hungers. It sustained Enoch as he saw generation after generation pass away in "wars and bloodshed" (Moses 7:16). The Lord told Enoch "all the doings of the children of men; . . . and [Enoch] looked upon their wickedness, and their misery, and wept" (Moses 7:41). But after seeing the redemption of Christ, Enoch "received a fulness of joy" (Moses 7:67). The peace of the gospel sustained Paul through all his trials, leading him to exclaim:

> Who shall separate us from the love of Christ? shall tribulation, or distress, or persecution, or famine, or nakedness, or peril, or sword? . . .
>
> Nay, in all these things we are more than conquerors through him that loved us.
>
> For I am persuaded, that neither death, nor life, nor angels, nor principalities, nor powers, nor things present, nor things to come,
>
> Nor height, nor depth, nor any other creature, shall be able to separate us from the love of God, which is in Christ Jesus our Lord. (Romans 8:35, 37–39.)

Jacob encouraged his people to endure "the crosses of the world," promising them that "their joy shall be full forever" (2 Nephi 9:18). The Lord's words to the persecuted and driven Missouri Saints echo these promises: "And all they who suffer persecution for my name, and endure in faith, though they are called to lay down their lives for my sake yet shall they partake of all this glory. Wherefore, fear not even unto death; for in this world your joy is not full, but in me your joy is full." (D&C 101:35–36.)

It is important to constantly remember the Lord's commandment to be joyful. The promise of a "fulness of joy" that the Lord extends to the faithful followers of righteousness should be ever present in our minds. It is critical for Latter-day Saints especially to let these teachings sink deep in their hearts, for we live in a time of trial, temptation, fear, and growing evil. We do not want to assume the dark, negative posture of the world, but rather should radiate the glory of the gospel's joys.

It is striking that the Lord introduced the Restoration with Isaiah's prophesy that "a *marvelous* work is about to come forth among the children of men" (D&C 4:1). This is repeated in numerous sections of the Doctrine and Covenants. The gospel truly is "great and marvelous" in that it instills hope and joy in the hearts of all who accept it, even in the most difficult of times. "Wherefore, I the Lord, knowing the calamity which should come upon the inhabitants of the earth, called upon my servant Joseph Smith, Jun., . . . and gave him commandments" (D&C 1:17). These commandments radiate love and will produce happiness in the lives of those who live them. Then let the "calamity" come. We have been prepared.

The scriptures testify that another fulness will grow in the last days—the fulness of iniquity. It is inspired by the adversary, who "seeketh that all men might be miserable like unto himself" (2 Nephi 2:27). This book will describe Satan's "fulness." It is important, however, that we learn of his fulness and ponder the declining character of our society against the backdrop of the promised fulness of joy. The "calamity" must be studied in the context of the "great and marvelous work." The Latter-day Saints are not prophets of doom. There may be tests, trials, and sorrows waiting, but they need not bring us to despair. Alma once prayed: "May God grant unto you that your burdens may be light, through the joy of his Son. And even all this can ye do if ye will." (Alma 33:23.) In the last dark days of the Nephites, Mormon also encouraged his son, Moroni, with thoughts of the Savior "and the hope of his glory and of eternal life." May these thoughts "rest in your mind forever," he wrote (Moroni 9:25).

This book will also examine the fulness of light and truth. It will describe through the scriptures the pathway that leads to it, for only in a fulness of light and truth can joy and happiness be eternally sustained. Latter-day Saints must walk the pathway of light and truth if they expect to build Zion. We need not fear, for Zion will be built. It is up to us as individuals to participate in its establishment.

The relationship of these fulnesses of light and truth is seen in the experience of King Lamoni. In a small way his experience is representative of all times and all people. In Alma 19 we read:

Now, this was what Ammon desired, for he knew that king Lamoni was under the power of God; he knew that the dark veil of unbelief was being cast away from his mind, and the light which did light up his mind, which was the light of the glory of God, which was a marvelous light of his goodness—yea, this light had infused such joy into his soul, the cloud of darkness having been dispelled, and that the light of everlasting life was lit up in his soul, yea, he knew that this had overcome his natural frame, and he was carried away in God (Alma 19:6).

The scriptures testify that Lamoni's experience can be shared by all, and that prior to the Second Coming the whole world will be cleansed by "the light of everlasting life." John the Revelator promises that eventually "God shall wipe away all tears from their eyes; and there shall be no more death, neither sorrow, nor crying, neither shall there be any more pain: for the former things are passed away" (Revelation 21:4). The "tree of life" will "[yield] her fruit every month: and the leaves of the tree" will be "for the healing of the nations" (Revelation 22:2).

I have tasted of the fruit of the tree of life and have found the words of the angel to Nephi to be true. It is "the most joyous to the soul" (1 Nephi 11:23). It is "sweet above all that is sweet, . . . white above all that is white, yea, and pure above all that is pure." It is indeed "most precious," and I have been "filled, that [I] hunger not, . . . neither [do I] thirst" (Alma 32:42). That joy sustains me as I watch with growing dismay the decay of my society as it dwindles into a fulness of iniquity. It encourages and lifts me as I strive to obtain a fulness of light and truth by following the Savior—the master of joy and happiness.

2

THE FULNESS OF INIQUITY:
SCRIPTURAL WARNINGS

A NUMBER OF YEARS AGO, I found myself alone one New Year's Eve. It was a rare occasion; I would not spend this night with my family, and I was rather melancholy. With nothing better to do, I turned on the television just in time to catch a special program by one of the networks reviewing the events of the past year. For half an hour the major news stories of the year were detailed. I was amazed at the vast number of things that had occurred in a single year, but what shocked me most was the central theme of sorrow, despair, and pain that ran throughout the stories portrayed. A few minutes into the program I was weeping at the sad music of humanity as it inflicted upon itself so much more than mankind was ever meant to bear.

As I pondered the scenes that passed before me I could not help but recall a statement made by Mormon describing his own world when he said: "a continual scene of wickedness and abominations has been before mine eyes ever since I have been sufficient to behold the ways of man" (Mormon 2:18). As I have reviewed the conditions of the world and particularly of our own beloved American nation, it has been impressed upon my mind that there exists a haunting familiarity between our own generation and those societies described in the scriptures who reached a condition the Book of Mormon calls "the fulness of iniquity."

I have discovered that the Lord never describes a problem in the scriptures, particularly a problem that is deeply relevant to our own situation, whether individual or societal, without also detailing the solution. Even if the broader society rejects his counsels, we as individuals can receive comfort, hope, and direction for ourselves and families. We need not fear or be negative, we need only trust in the Lord's wisdom and apply his counsel. This is especially true for people who face the specific challenges of living in a world that is slipping deeper and deeper into the fulness of iniquity.

Several years ago, while teaching Genesis 15, I came across a phrase that demanded closer study. Here the Lord reiterates to Abraham the promise that Abraham's seed will inherit the land of Canaan. He then informs Abraham of the future Egyptian captivity. As if in explanation of the long captivity, the Lord adds, "But in the fourth generation they shall come hither again: for the iniquity of the Amorites is not yet full" (Genesis 15:16).

This passage prompted me to search ancient scriptural civilizations to understand what constitutes "the fulness of iniquity." In Abraham's time the Canaanites had not yet reached that "fulness"; therefore, the Israelites could not inherit the land. That inheritance came after the Canaanites were deserving of destruction.

The Decrees of God

When Moroni abridged the Jaredite records, he paused in his narrative to give our generation a warning. Reflecting on his own destroyed civilization and that of the Jaredites, Moroni explained the decree that prevails over the Americans:

> For behold, this is a land which is choice above all other lands; wherefore he that doth possess it shall serve God or shall be swept off; for it is the everlasting decree of God. And it is not until the fulness of iniquity among the children of the land, that they are swept off.
>
> And this cometh unto you, O ye Gentiles, that ye may

know the decrees of God—that ye may repent, and not continue in your iniquities until the fulness come, that ye may not bring down the fulness of the wrath of God upon you as the inhabitants of the land have hitherto done. (Ether 2:10–11.)

At the beginning of Nephite civilization Lehi contemplated a vision he received of the destruction of Jerusalem (2 Nephi 1:4). He projected that bitter lesson to his new land, warning his sons of the "decrees of God" concerning the promised land. If they remained true to their God, Lehi admonished, no country or power on earth could take the land from them; but "if iniquity shall abound cursed shall be the land for their sakes, but unto the righteous it shall be blessed forever" (2 Nephi 1:7).

Throughout Nephite history Book of Mormon prophets taught their people of this decree. Alma said, "There is a curse upon all this land, that destruction shall come upon all those workers of darkness . . . when they are fully ripe" (Alma 37:28). He also taught, "Cursed shall be the land . . . unto every nation, kindred, tongue, and people, unto destruction, which do wickedly, when they are fully ripe" (Alma 45:16).

The scripture quoted from Ether shows evidence that Moroni knew the seeds that would blossom as the fulness of iniquity would be part of "gentile" society. He specifically warned the latter-day Gentiles not to "continue" in their iniquities until the fulness is reached, implying that the gentile society would also be swept off the land. In light of Moroni's warning, these words of the Lord to Joseph Smith take on added meaning: "Mine indignation is soon to be poured out without measure upon all nations; and this will I do when the cup of their iniquity is full" (D&C 101:11). In another revelation the Lord described the state of the earth by saying, "All flesh is corrupted before me; and the powers of darkness prevail upon the earth, among the children of men . . . which causeth silence to reign, and all eternity is pained, and the angels are waiting the great command to reap down the earth, to gather the tares that they may be burned" (D&C 38:11–12).

If this description was true in 1831 it is certainly true today. Evidently the nations will have reached a fulness before the Second Coming, and their destruction will be the result. Thus, an understanding of the fulness of iniquity can give us a yard-stick to measure the "signs of the times" and the coming of the Lord.

Seven "Fulness" Societies

Is it possible to reduce the general term *fulness of iniquity* into specific evils, to break it down into workable terms for closer examination? If so, one could identify the behaviors within a society that lead to its destruction when "continued." One could know the enemy and be better prepared to meet him.

The scriptures contain many examples of peoples de-stroyed because of wickedness. In the next few chapters we will study seven such societies:

1. The generation of the Flood
2. The Jaredites
3. The Nephites of Mormon's time
4. Sodom and Gomorrah
5. The Canaanites prior to Joshua's conquest
6. The Israelites before their captivity and scattering
7. The Nephites before the coming of Christ, with special emphasis on the city of Ammonihah

Our study will examine statements by the Lord condemn-ing specific evils in each society and will link these evils directly to the coming destruction. A correlation of these state-ments by the Lord, and of common influences noted among the seven societies, will provide a broad picture of the fulness of iniquity. Seven behaviors that lead to the fulness of iniquity will emerge.

3

THE FULNESS OF INIQUITY:
OUTWARD SIGNS

VIOLENCE IN A SOCIETY IS AN outward sign of the coming fulness of iniquity.

The Generation of the Flood—Violence

Before the Flood the Lord gave Noah a specific reason for the coming destruction. The reason is identical in Genesis and Moses: the people were destroyed because the world was "filled with *violence*" (Moses 8:20–30; Genesis 6:11–13, italics added). Violent sins are in a category of their own. It requires no imagination to understand this type of sin. However, we will refine this term as we study the other societies. Specific acts of violence will be revealed, as will the people, both individuals and groups, who are the common victims of violence.

The evil of violence is stressed over and over again by Old Testament prophets. Isaiah warns his people that "their works are works of iniquity, and the act of violence is in their hands" (Isaiah 59:6). A generation later Jeremiah mourns, "Violence and spoil is heard in her [Jerusalem]; before me continually is grief and wounds" (Jeremiah 6:7). "But thine eyes and thine heart are not but for thy covetousness, . . . and for oppression, and for violence, to do it" (Jeremiah 22:17). Ezekiel writes that "violence is risen up into a rod of wickedness" (Ezekiel 7:11). Micah decries the "rich men . . . full of violence" (Micah 6:12). Amos condemns those "who store up violence and robbery in their palaces" (Amos 3:10). Even Jonah describes this trait among the Ninevites, with one exception—they repent. The king exhorts his people to "turn every one from his evil way, and from violence that is in their hands" (Jonah 3:8). Habakkuk cries "of violence" unto the Lord, asking the Lord, "Why dost thou shew me iniquity, and cause me to behold grievance? for spoiling and violence are before me" (Habakkuk 1:2–3).

It is not difficult to see this trait in our own society. It is sad that younger and younger people are becoming not only the victims of an increasingly violent society but also are beginning to perpetuate acts of violence. Violence in our society is often mistakenly associated with courage and manhood. A closer examination, however, reveals that the more wicked a people or person becomes the more they equate cowardice with courage. Drive-by shootings, terrorist acts, ethnic cleansing of villages, etc, are all essentially performed by cowards masquerading in the dress of bravery.

Many acts of violence are committed by various criminal elements in the nation. This brings us to another influence, which is explained in Moroni's commentary on Jaredite society.

The Jaredites—Secret Combinations

As he did in Ether 2, Moroni interrupts his narrative of Jaredite history to give a specific warning to future gentile generations. This warning calls attention to the reason behind the destruction of the Jaredite and the Nephite civilizations. Speaking of secret combinations, Moroni indicates that "they have caused the destruction of this people of whom I am now speaking, and also the destruction of the people of Nephi." Moroni then projects this ultimate destruction to any nation that "shall uphold such secret combinations, to get power and gain, until they shall spread over the nation." This is followed by a direct warning to the Gentiles so that they "may repent of [their] sins, and suffer not that these murderous combinations shall get above [them]." (Ether 8:20–23.)

A brief study of the scriptures reveals much concerning the organization and objectives of secret combinations. The following scriptural statements illuminate the nature of secret combinations:

1. They are "among all people" (Ether 8:20).
2. They seek "power and gain" (Ether 8:22) and the "glory of the world" (Helaman 7:5).
3. They seek "to overthrow the freedom of all lands, nations, and countries" (Ether 8:25). This is the specific warning to the latter-day peoples of the Americas.
4. They are "built up by the devil" (Ether 8:25).
5. They "combine against all righteousness," and specifically "against the people of the Lord" (3 Nephi 6:28–29).
6. They seek to "deliver those who [are] guilty . . . from the grasp of justice" (3 Nephi 6:29).
7. They "set at defiance the law and rights of their country" (3 Nephi 6:30).
8. They enter into oaths of secrecy bound by "their heads" (Moses 5:29).
9. They live by Cain's three principles (Moses 5:31, 33, 34):
   a. "I may murder and get gain." (Mahan Principle: life for money.)
   b. "I am free" (I can sin and not have to pay the consequences.)
   c. "Am I my brother's keeper?" (I have no responsibility to my fellowman. Social Darwinism, also expressed by Korihor in Alma 30:17.)
10. They claim to be "avenging the wrongs of those that had received no wrong, save it were they had wronged themselves" (3 Nephi 3:11).
11. They "keep [the people] in darkness" (Ether 8:16).
12. They "commit many murders, and . . . do much slaughter among the people" (3 Nephi 1:27). They "slay . . . many people, and . . . lay waste . . . many cities, and . . .

spread . . . much death and carnage throughout the land" (3 Nephi 2:11).

The most traditional interpretation of a secret combination is organized crime. A better description would be organized evil. Any ideology, government, business, or other organization or system that makes "power and gain" its objective and uses illegal, immoral, or unethical means to achieve those ends should be considered a secret combination. Moroni said that "they are had among all people" (Ether 8:20). These secret combinations use violence to obtain "power and gain," as the scriptural record shows. Violence is the lowest common denominator of all secret combinations, from Cain to the Gadianton robbers.

An interesting feature of Moroni's warning to the Gentiles of the latter days is found in Ether 8. In verse 24 there is a shift in number from *secret combinations* (plural) to *secret combination* (singular). The specific goal of this "secret combination" will be to "overthrow the freedom of all lands, . . . and it bringeth to pass the destruction of all people" (Ether 8:25). Perhaps this number change is not significant; Moroni may be referring to the totality of Satan's kingdom in the last days. Or perhaps he is referring to a specific, single organization in the last days that will be instrumental in overthrowing freedom and leading the world to the destructions prophesied before the advent of the Savior.

Whether a single secret combination "spreads over the land" or numerous criminal secret combinations "spread over the land," the result is the same. In our own time it could well be a combination of the two forces. The society that allows these combinations—either an individual one (such as communism) or a multiplicity of smaller ones (such as organized crime and gangs; corrupt judges, politicians, and public officials; colluding businessmen; self-serving associations; and even general public passion for material wealth)—to "spread over the nation" until they "get above you" will reach the fulness of iniquity.

The Nephites of Mormon's Time—"Without Civilization"

A letter from Mormon to Moroni reveals additional reasons for the Nephite fall. After describing the atrocities of the Lamanites, Mormon writes of the depravity of his own people. "Many of the daughters of the Lamanites have they taken prisoners," Mormon relates. "And after depriving them of that which was most dear and precious above all things, which is chastity and virtue, . . . they did murder them in a most cruel manner, torturing their bodies even unto death; and after they have done this, they devour their flesh like unto wild beasts" (Moroni 9:9–10). Mormon concludes his description of Nephite violence by questioning, "How can we expect that God will stay his hand in judgment against us?" (Verse 14.) The phrase Mormon uses to capsulize these actions is "without civilization" (verse 11). This is an excellent phrase for the fulness of iniquity.

Other phrases follow which give a perspective on the meaning of "without civilization." Mormon speaks of "awful brutality." The people are "without order and without mercy"; they are full of "perversion" and "brutal"; they are "without principle, and past feeling." (Moroni 9:17–20.) The normal human restraints on the "natural man," such as mercy, compassion, sympathy, and justice, have been removed from Nephite society.

Mormon tells Moroni that a Nephite army under the command of Zenephi has carried away the few provisions the Lamanites left the Nephite widows and daughters. These same widows were earlier victims of Lamanite atrocities. The Nephite army "left them to wander withersoever they [could] for food; and many old women [did] faint by the way and die" (Moroni 9:16). Apparently the Lamanites at least left a few provisions for the old women and girls to subsist on, even though they were their enemies. The Nephites stripped them of all, showing a complete lack of mercy. They were "without civilization."

Concluding this section of his letter, Mormon states that

"the suffering of our women and our children upon all the face of this land doth exceed everything; yea, tongue cannot tell, neither can it be written" (Moroni 9:19). He alludes to the Jaredites, who also committed such acts before their destruction.

A close examination of this letter reveals who the victims of man's loss of civilization most often are. It was the women and children to whom the Lamanites fed the flesh of their husbands and fathers. It was the "Lamanite daughters" who were tortured and murdered. It was the "widows and their daughters" who "faint[ed] by the way and die[d]." It was women and children who fell "victims to their awful brutality" when they fled to the army of Aaron. Remember Mormon's concluding observation: "The suffering of our women and our children upon all the face of this land doth exceed everything."

A people have reached the fulness of iniquity when they have lost the normal human qualities that prevent them from victimizing each other, particularly women and children, in such a brutal and violent manner. This is not only evil; it is unnatural and perverted. There is a natural civilizing impulse in all human beings that teaches that we do not abuse, harm, exploit, or brutalize women, children, the aged, and so on. But when a society ceases to make these civilizing distinctions a flood of violence is the result. The Nephites victimized each of these groups. A quick examination of this trait in conjunction with the two already discussed shows a ready correlation. Secret combinations using violent means lead to the victimizing of women and children, who are often the least able to defend themselves in a society. These evils eloquently combine in a warning Moroni gives to the societies of the last days when he asks, "Why do ye build up your secret abominations to get gain, and cause that widows should mourn before the Lord, and also orphans to mourn before the Lord, and also the blood of their fathers and their husbands to cry unto the Lord from the ground, for vengeance upon your heads?" (Mormon 8:40.)

One of the most insidious of evils relating to women and children comes in the form of pornography. This problem has existed in our nation for some time, but more recently child pornography has become epidemic. The more this is allowed to spread, the closer we come to imitating the sins of Sodom and Gomorrah.

Sodom and Gomorrah—Perversion of the Procreative Gift

For many, Sodom and Gomorrah represent the epitome of destroyed societies. Their legacy to the world remains in the word *sodomy*, which in general terms represents the perverted use of the procreative power God gave to man. An examination of Lot's experience in Sodom reveals one facet of this perverted usage: homosexuality. The Lord declares to Abraham that "the cry of Sodom and Gomorrah is great" and that "their sin is very grievous" (Genesis 18:20). The grievousness of their sin is expressed by Jude in a clear, concise statement: because Sodom and Gomorrah gave "themselves over to fornication, and [went] after strange flesh," they "are set forth for an example, suffering the vengeance of eternal fire" (Jude 1:7).

Jude's phrase, "giving themselves over" suggests two things. The society becomes obsessed with sexual matters. It also gives in to sexual desires without any guides or standards to control them.

The fulness of iniquity encompasses "fornication" and the perverted use of God's procreative power ("going after strange flesh"). In conjunction with other traits, this perversion often takes the violent forms detailed in Lot's experience in Sodom and Mormon's descriptions of his people. Secret combinations use these perversions to obtain power and gain. Women and children are most often the victims. The Israelite apostasy surrounded the immoral practices of the "groves." Amos put it bluntly when he condemned his people by saying, "A man and his father will go in unto the same maid" (Amos 2:7). In light of Amos's words it is interesting that a modern, very popular adolescent movie jokingly made light of a father and son having an immoral relationship with the same woman. Ezekiel described the environment that is conducive to a licentious society. It is hauntingly familiar to our own. "Behold, this was the iniquity of thy sister Sodom, pride, fulness of bread, and abundance of idleness" (Ezekiel 16:49).

Early in Nephite history the men of Jacob's time wished to practice plural marriage for immoral reasons. The Lord "delights in the chastity of women," Jacob told them, "and whoredoms are an abomination before me" (Jacob 2:28). Jacob then warned them that the specific sins they were contemplating would bring on their eventual destruction by the Lamanites. "The Lamanites which are not filthy like unto you . . . shall scourge you even unto destruction. And the time speedily cometh that except ye repent they shall possess the land of your inheritance, and the Lord God will lead away the righteous out from among you." (Jacob 3:3–4.) Jacob then told his people that the Lord would be "merciful" to the Lamanites because of their observance of the law of chastity.

A full description of these types of perversions is provided in the Lord's assessment of the Canaanites also. Because of the perverted nature of this evil, detailed discussion is inappropriate; however, the Canaanites provide us with another aspect of a fulness-of-iniquity society.

The Canaanites—Fascination with Evil

Before the children of Israel entered the promised land, Moses gathered them together and gave them his last charge. In that charge are found the keys to both Canaanite and Israelite destruction. In Leviticus 18, Moses warns the children of Israel against the abominations of the Canaanites: "After the doings of the land of Canaan, whither I bring you, shall ye not do" (Leviticus 18:3). Following this injunction, Moses details the immoral perversions of a society that has reached the fulness of iniquity. He warns, "Defile not ye yourselves in any of these things: for in all these the nations are defiled which I cast out before you: . . . and the land itself vomiteth out her inhabitants" (Leviticus 18:24—25).

In Deuteronomy Moses gives another specific reason for the Canaanite expulsion:

There shall not be found among you any one that maketh his son or his daughter to pass through the fire, or that useth divination, or an observer of times, or an enchanter, or a witch,

Or a charmer, or a consulter with familiar spirits, or a wizard, or a necromancer.

For all that do these things are an abomination unto the Lord: and because of these abominations the Lord thy God doth drive them out from before thee. (Deuteronomy 18:10–12.)

These iniquities have a common theme: that of the occult or a fascination with evil for the sake of evil. This indicator of the fulness of iniquity has a direct tie with the adversary and his kingdom. It is also evidenced by a fascination with death, blood, and so forth. Evidences of this characteristic were found among the Nephites. Mormon reported "that there were sorceries, and witchcrafts, and magics; and the power of the evil one was wrought upon all the face of the land" (Mormon 1:19). In his letter to Moroni, Mormon described his people as "delighting in so much abomination" and "delighting in everything save that which is good" (Moroni 9:13,19).

Isaiah warns the Israelites about seeking "unto them that have familiar spirits, and unto wizards that peep, and that mutter" (Isaiah 8:19). In the generation of Noah "every imagination of the thoughts of [man's] heart was only evil continually" (Genesis 6:5; see also Moses 8:22). All point to a fascination and a "delight" with evil for evil's sake. People are aware that what they are doing is evil and as Cain "gloried in his wickedness" (Moses 5:31), they find pleasure in their own perversions. This characteristic accompanies violence, for that is often the road the occult takes as it invites perversions of the procreative gift, loss of human restraint, and other serious sins.

This trait of a fulness-of-iniquity society is readily seen in the mass media industry. It is pervasive in much of rock music and in popular television and movies. It is also seen in modern society's fascination with crime. Joseph F. Smith warned the saints of this tendency many years ago. "Young men may please God by thinking right, by acting right, by shunning, as they would destruction, not only every crime, but the spirit either to see . . . or to hear or read the details of his damnable acts" (*Gospel Doctrine*, Deseret Book Co., 1977, p. 375). We increasingly hear the debate regarding the link between evil themes in movies, books, or music and their impact on the actions of those who participate in them. President Smith commented on this matter also. "It was Shelley who said that 'strange thoughts beget strange deeds,' and when our children are reading books that are creating strange and unusual and undesirable thoughts in their minds we need not be surprised to learn that they have committed some unusual, some strange, or unnatural act" (*Gospel Doctrine*, pp. 324–25).

The evils described in this chapter are overt, outward signs of the fulness of iniquity. They are interrelated and feed each other. Their combined weight has brought down major civilizations.

In the next chapters we will examine evil influences that are attitudinal in nature and often more difficult to detect than violence, secret combinations, and the others we have considered. Nonetheless, they are just as insidious and must not be "continued."

4

The Israelites' Worship of False Gods

DEUTERONOMY INCLUDES MANY of Moses's warnings to Israel that are prophetic in nature. These warnings contain a sixth key to understanding the fulness of iniquity. This key—when added to violence, secret combinations, victimization of women and children, perverted immorality, and a fascination with evil—brings into sharper focus the danger facing modern society.

A Mosaic Warning

Moses wrote:

> When thou shalt beget children, and children's children, and ye shall have remained long in the land, and shall corrupt yourselves, and make a graven image, or the likeness of any thing, and shall do evil in the sight of the Lord thy God, to provoke him to anger:
>
> I call heaven and earth to witness against you this day, that ye shall soon utterly perish from off the land whereunto ye go over Jordan to possess it; ye shall not prolong your days upon it, but shall utterly be destroyed. (Deuteronomy 4:25–26.)

The fear that his people would worship false gods is so pressing on Moses's mind that he repeats his prophetic warning later in the same book: "If thou do at all forget the Lord thy God, and walk after other gods, and serve them, and worship them," Moses testifies, ". . . ye shall surely perish. As the nations which the Lord destroyeth before your face, so shall ye perish; because ye would not be obedient unto the voice of the Lord your God." (Deuteronomy 8:19–20.) In this verse Moses adds the concept of disobedience, linking it with the worship of false gods. Disobedience to the Lord proved to be the downfall of Israel. A close look at the Old Testament reveals two main false gods Israel worshipped that were not represented by stone carvings. Baal, Ashtaroth, and Molech were certainly evil, and their worship fostered the influences already mentioned. However, Israel's downfall came with the worship of other, less obvious, gods dominant in wicked societies, ancient and modern.

The Arm of Flesh—Materialism and Military Might

In the Old Testament prophetic messages, especially Isaiah's, before the Northern Kingdom's fall and the Southern Kingdom's captivity, one discovers a common, often-repeated theme. Whatever other warnings the prophets give, two ring out chapter after chapter: the Israelites are invoking the wrath of God by seeking security in (1) wealth and material prosperity (and are doing everything within their power, right or wrong, to get it) and in (2) military might and alliances with militaristic nations.

Forgotten by the Israelites is the truth that security comes in righteousness and in trust in the arm of Jehovah, not man. While it is true that readiness for defense was a critical factor in, for example, the Nephites' military successes, true security would exist when a nation's spiritual condition ensured the Lord's direct protection, making great armies, swords along the wall, or vast material wealth neither needed nor glorified. With striking imagery Jeremiah stresses the folly of seeking security in anything but the Lord: "My people have committed two evils; they have forsaken me the fountain of living waters, and hewed them out cisterns, broken cisterns, that can hold no water" (Jeremiah 2:13).

Consider the following counsel from Isaiah: "Their land also is full of silver and gold, neither is there any end of their treasures; their land is also full of horses, neither is there any end of their chariots" (Isaiah 2:7). Horses and chariots were the symbols of military might in the ancient world. Israel had few of them. In times of threat they often sought alliances with greater foreign powers. Thus Isaiah warned them not to "go down to Egypt for help; and stay on horses, and trust in chariots, because they are many; and in horsemen, because they are very strong." They were to "look . . . unto the Holy One of Israel" and "seek the Lord." (Isaiah 31:1.)

Isaiah fairly overflows with condemnation of the gluttony of "silver and gold" (Isaiah 2:7); the laying up of property by joining "house to house" (Isaiah 5:8); pride and haughtiness; the false sophistication of fashion among both men and women; and the oppression of the poor, the widows, and the fatherless, who are most often the victims of men's greed. Dishonest merchandising, bribery, military alliances, plans for conquests, and boasting in military strength are all condemned by the prophet.

Throughout his writings, Isaiah warns of the false security in the outward forms of religion by which the people think they can buy off the Lord. What is needed is justice, judgment, and relief of the burdens of those in need. But in a society where everything can be bought and sold, people believe that even the Lord's favor is up for sale. In a society searching for wealth and power there is never an end, a final destination or goal, for no amount of either is satisfying. Isaiah warns, "They are greedy dogs which can never have enough, . . . they all look to their own way, every one for his gain, from his quarter" (Isaiah 56:11). Specifying why Israel was smitten, the Lord sums up all in a single word: "For the iniquity of his *covetousness* was I wroth, and smote him" (Isaiah 57:17). Jeremiah echoes the same thoughts on the eve of Judah's captivity: "For from the least of them even unto the greatest of them every one is given to covetousness" (Jeremiah 6:13).

Time and space do not permit me to detail the teachings of

all the prophets, but the same themes occupy a major portion of prophetic writing. At the time of the Savior the same problems plagued Israel. His greatest display of indignation came when he witnessed the buying and selling and the making of profit in the temple. The final act that brought a speedy destruction less than forty years after the Resurrection was the rejection of the true God of Israel in favor of the zealous military messiahs that brought the madness and self-destruction of A.D. 70 and 132.

The Oppression of the Poor

A result of a society's emphasis on materialism and war is often the oppression of the poor, the "widows and fatherless," so often spoken of in the scriptures. Indeed, the oppression or neglect of the poor could almost stand as an independent key to the fulness of iniquity. It goes hand in hand with the prophetic denunciation of covetousness. Ezekiel condemns Jerusalem's neglect of the poor and links it with the coming destruction:

> Behold, this was the iniquity of thy sister Sodom, pride, fulness of bread, and abundance of idleness was in her and in her daughters, neither did she strengthen the hand of the poor and needy.
> And they were haughty, and committed abomination before me: therefore I took them away as I saw good. (Ezekiel 16:49–50.)

Ezekiel later returns to this theme, linking it with "lewdness," "dishonest gain," "shedding blood," "violated law," and other evils. Ezekiel condemns "the people of the land" for using "oppression" and "robbery" and for vexing "the poor and needy: yea, they have oppressed the stranger wrongfully" (Ezekiel 22:29). It is significant that Ezekiel mentions an "abundance of idleness" as a sin that is related to wealth, pride, and the neglect of the poor. Idleness also leads to the other sins common in a "fulness" society.

Amos also includes the treatment of the poor in his list of specific sins that caused Israel's downfall. The Lord tells Israel that he "will not turn away the punishment thereof; because they sold the righteous for silver, and the poor for a pair of shoes; that pant after the dust of the earth on the head of the poor, and turn aside the way of the meek" (Amos 2:6–7). He returns again to the poor later in his writing. The people "oppress the poor" and "crush the needy" (Amos 4:1). They "[tread] . . . upon the poor" and "turn aside the poor in the gate from their right" (Amos 5:11–12). The worldly men of Amos's time

> swallow up the needy, even to make the poor of the land to fail,
>
> Saying, When will the new moon be gone, that we may sell corn? and the sabbath, that we may set forth wheat, making the ephah small, and the shekel great, and falsifying the balances by deceit?
>
> That we may buy the poor for silver, and the needy for a pair of shoes; yea, and sell the refuse of the wheat? (Amos 8:4–6.)

Jeremiah speaks of a specific kind of treatment of the poor, an injustice that often has no defense. He criticizes the man "that buildeth his house by unrighteousness, and his chambers by wrong; that useth his neighbor's service without wages, and giveth him not for his work" (Jeremiah 22:13). Following this condemnation Jeremiah tells the people it will be "well" with them when they "[judge] the cause of the poor and needy" (Jeremiah 22:15–16). In similar manner Daniel promises Nebuchadnezzar that he can "break off thy sins by righteousness, and thine iniquities by shewing mercy to the poor" (Daniel 4:27).

Micah links violence and covetousness with the oppression of the poor. In his generation the rich took "fields . . . by violence; and houses, . . . so they oppress a man and his house, even a man and his heritage" (Micah 2:2). Isaiah continually speaks on this theme, showing the indignation of the Lord toward the rich because "the spoil of the poor is in [their] houses" and because they "beat my people to pieces, and grind the faces of the poor" (Isaiah 3:14–15). One of the last straws before the Babylonian captivity in the days of Jeremiah was the unwillingness of the wealthy to release the poor from their debts. Ironically, since they insisted on keeping their brethren financially captive, they themselves went into captivity. (See Jeremiah 34).

The Book of Mormon's Witness

An elementary reading of the Book of Mormon quickly reveals that at times the Nephite society worshipped the same two gods, materialism and military might, and that they treated the poor accordingly. The desire to conquer militarily is the deciding factor that ends Nephite society. The lust for conquest and revenge causes Mormon to "utterly refuse from this time forth to be a . . . leader of this people" (Mormon 3:11). After winning a victory over the Lamanites "they began to boast in their own strength, . . . and they did swear . . . that they would go up to battle against their enemies, and would cut them off from the face of the land" (Mormon 3:9–10).

An offensive attack upon the Lamanites ends in defeat, bringing forth Mormon's commentary:

> It was because the armies of the Nephites went up unto the Lamanites that they began to be smitten; for were it not for that, the Lamanites could have had no power over them.
> But, behold, the judgments of God will overtake the wicked; and it is by the wicked that the wicked are punished; for it is the wicked that stir up the hearts of the children of men unto bloodshed. (Mormon 4:4–5.)

Similar emphasis on offensive warfare and conquering is apparent among King Noah's people. They too "were lifted up in the pride of their hearts; they did boast in their own strength, saying that their fifty could stand against thousands of the Lamanites." Not only did they boast, but they "did delight in blood, and the shedding of the blood of their brethren" (Mosiah 11:19).

Forgotten by both these peoples and others in the Book of Mormon was the Lord's counsel "never to give an offense, yea, and never to raise the sword . . . except it were to preserve their lives" (Alma 48:14). In so doing they were promised the Lord's intervention in their behalf. This principle was not neglected by the Nephites' greatest military captain, Moroni. After a great battle, he ascribed the victory to the Lord's preservation and the people's righteousness. "I would that ye should understand," he tells the Lamanite leader, "that this is done unto us because of our religion and our faith in Christ" (Alma 44:3). Book of Mormon emphasis on this war theme is extensive, but victory is always ascribed to the Lord's protection of righteous, unified people, not to military strength.

The madness of militarism works out most tragically in the insane designs of the last Jaredite leaders and their armies as opposing forces among them frantically try to defeat each other. Their hatred and their lust for conquest leads to mutual annihilation, proving that "by the wicked . . . the wicked are punished" (Mormon 4:5).

John described the bloodthirsty nature of men in the last days with symbolic language. The sea, the rivers, and fountains of water are turned to blood, reminiscent of one of the plagues of Egypt. An angel witnessing this proclaims: "Thou art righteous, O Lord . . . because thou hast judged thus. For they have shed the blood of saints and prophets, and thou hast given them blood to drink; for they are worthy." (Revelation 16:5–6.)

Just prior to his martyrdom, Joseph Smith was approached by some militia leaders. During their conversation he uttered a prophecy that helps to explain John's imagery. Although his words were specifically directed toward the Civil War, their application has wider ramifications. "I can see what is in your hearts and I will tell you what I see. I can see that you thirst for blood, and nothing but my blood will satisfy you. . . . And inasmuch as you and the people thirst for blood, I prophesy, in the name of the Lord, that you shall witness scenes of blood and sorrow to your entire satisfaction. Your souls shall be perfectly satiated with blood, and many of you who are now present shall have an opportunity to face the cannon's mouth from sources you think not of; and those people that desire this great evil upon me and my brethren, shall be filled with regret and sorrow because of the scenes of desolation and distress that await them. They shall seek for peace and not be able to find it." (DHC vol. 6, p. 566.)

The Book of Mormon reveals in detail the second false god, materialism—the worshipping of wealth as an end in itself—and its companion evil of neglect of the poor. The prosperity-pride-wickedness-destruction-humility cycle repeats itself with astonishing frequency through the succeeding generations. It is this stress on wealth that allows the Gadianton robbers to increase and take power so rapidly. The great Nephite peace after the visit of Christ is slowly eroded by the encroaching pride and class system created by the prosperity and wealth of the people. Everyone is busy acquiring "the fine things of the world" (4 Nephi 1:24). This same emphasis is seen in the Nephite civilization destroyed before Christ's coming. Though the Lord tries to warn them by making their riches "slippery" so they cannot firmly grasp them, they fail to catch the significance and continue to chase the vain promise of happiness and fulfillment through wealth. But these promises, like a wet bar of soap, could never be grasped securely.

As in the Old Testament, the treatment of the poor is included in the list of sins catalogued in the book of Helaman: "It was because of the pride of their hearts, because of their exceeding riches, . . . their oppression to the poor, withholding their food from the hungry, withholding their clothing from the naked, and smiting their humble brethren upon the cheek" that the Nephites lost the blessings and protection of the Lord (Helaman 4:12). The same book relates that the Gadianton robbers in their secret combinations "smite and rend and turn their backs upon the poor and the meek" (Helaman 6:39).

Every major Book of Mormon prophet speaks about the corrupting influence of wealth, knowing it would lead to the selfishness and greed inherent in "fulness" civilizations. Perhaps Mormon summed up this problem best when he wrote to Moroni saying, "Behold, the pride of this nation, or the people of the Nephites, hath proven their destruction" (Moroni 8:27).

A Modern Prophet's Witness

In each society we address, these two gods, materialism and militarism, appear; the examples are myriad. In the latter days a modern prophet, Spencer W. Kimball, has issued a similar warning in an address titled, prophetically, "The False Gods We Worship." In that discourse, published as the First Presidency message in the June 1976 Bicentennial issue of the *Ensign*, President Kimball identifies these two great gods as the main gods of modern society:

> The Lord has blessed us as a people with a prosperity unequaled in times past. . . . I am afraid that many of us have been surfeited with flocks and herds and acres and barns and wealth and have begun to worship them as false gods, and they have power over us. . . . Many people spend most of their time working in the service of a self-image that includes sufficient money, stocks, bonds, investment portfolios, property, credit cards, furnishings, automobiles, and the like to *guarantee* carnal security throughout, it is hoped, a long and happy life. (P. 4.)

President Kimball's use of the term *self-image* is strikingly similar to the Lord's words in his preface to the Doctrine and Covenants: "They seek not the Lord to establish his righteousness," the Lord says, "but every man walketh in his own way, and after the image of his own god, whose image is in the likeness of the world, and whose substance is that of an idol" (D&C 1:16). Thus the Lord himself describes the emphasis of modern society on the image of success. Does not that image include those things described by President Kimball? This same "image" is alluded to in Moroni's vision of the last days. "Ye do love money," he says, "more than ye love the poor and the needy" (Mormon 8:37).

The second half of President Kimball's article addresses itself to the second false god, military might, which also promises a false security:

> We are a warlike people, easily distracted from our assignment of preparing for the coming of the Lord. When enemies rise up, we commit vast resources to the fabrication of gods of stone and steel—ships, planes, missiles, fortifications—and depend on them for protection and deliverance. When threatened, we become anti-enemy instead of pro-kingdom of God. . . . We forget that if we are righteous the Lord will either not suffer our enemies to come upon us—and this is the special promise to the inhabitants of the land of the Americas—or he will fight our battles for us. (P. 6.)

The emphasis of this quotation is positive, based on trust in God, not weapons. It encourages love, not fear and hatred. Throughout the Book of Mormon, hatred, a desire for conquest, and lack of trust are frequently the causes of war. At times these attributes are manifested by both Lamanites and Nephites. During the final war they are the driving motives that lead to the Nephites' destruction, just as they had earlier led to the destruction of the Jaredites.

An Ironic Conclusion

These two false gods correspond perfectly with the aims of secret combinations—power and gain. The victims often are women and children. The use of violence is pervasive. The relationships with all the other evils previously discussed are many.

A quick survey of the seven societies reveals that most were destroyed by war brought on by their own iniquities. This is true of the Nephites, the Jaredites, the Canaanites, and the Israelites. What a true and fitting irony for those societies that seek security in military might! Speaking on this theme in relation to the Jaredites, Moroni concludes "that the Lord did visit them in the fulness of his wrath, and *their wickedness* and abominations *had prepared a way* for their everlasting destruction" (Ether 14:25; italics added). Not only do the wicked punish the wicked—they also punish themselves. This truth is taught in the same context by Jeremiah. He told Israel that "thine own wickedness shall correct thee, and thy backslidings shall reprove thee" (Jeremiah 2:19).

Nephi testified that "the blood of that great and abominable church, . . . shall turn upon their own heads; for they shall war among themselves, and the sword of their own hands shall fall upon their own heads, and they shall be drunken with their own blood" (1 Nephi 22:13). This correlates perfectly with a Doctrine and Covenants description of the last days. Safety will be found only in Zion, for "it shall come to pass among the wicked, that every man that will not take his sword against his neighbor must needs flee unto Zion for safety. . . . And it shall be the only people that shall not be at war one with another." (D&C 45:68–69.)

Also ironic is the inability of "dwindling" societies to hold the wealth they seek. Their riches become "slippery," says the Book of Mormon, that the people "cannot hold them" (Helaman 13:36). In a society of secret combinations, wars, violence, and perversion, every person's hand will be against his neighbor and in his neighbor's pockets. Isaiah describes the slippery nature of wealth to his own generation. "No man shall spare his brother," he warns. "He shall snatch on the right hand, and be hungry; and he shall eat on the left hand, and they shall not be satisfied: they shall eat every man the flesh of his own arm." (Isaiah 9:19–20.)

The Lord has often warned his children not to trust in the "arm of flesh." It is foolish to do so, not only because true security is not found there, but also, as the scriptures teach, the arm of flesh is self-destructive. The attitudes that accompany the glorification of wealth and military might are an integral part of a "fulness" society. Their influence is hard to detect, because money and strength are not in and of themselves evil. Few societies, however, know how to use them for the benefit and true protection of man.

5

THE NEPHITES'
REJECTION OF THE GOOD

WE WILL NOW CONSIDER the seventh indicator that a society has reached the fulness of iniquity: its rejection of all that is good. We have saved this one for last, because it is both the initiator of the previously discussed iniquities and the last sign that the fulness has arrived.

Ammonihah and Zarahemla

Alma and Amulek's teachings to the city of Ammonihah introduce the rejection of the righteous. Ammonihah exhibits all the signs of an approaching fulness. The wicked citizens and rulers burn the believing women and children and also the scriptures in an act of semi-mob violence. Even before this event an angel warns Alma that the people of Ammonihah "do study at this time that they may destroy the liberty of thy people" (Alma 8:17). This statement, linked with the description of the city's lawyers in Alma 11:20, indicates a society based on wealth and prestige where bribery, violence, and dishonesty are common. Their scoffing at the notion that "this great city should be destroyed in one day" (Alma 9:4) suggests a sense of security in military might. Yet in spite of this iniquity, there is still a spark of hope. One last step remains to be taken before Ammonihah reaches a fulness. The burning of the women, children, and scriptures, coupled with the stoning of the men who accept Alma and Amulek's message, indicate that the people are taking this last step. Amulek makes this connection explicit in his warning to his friends and neighbors:

> If it were not for the prayers of the righteous, . . . ye would
> even now be visited with utter destruction. . . .
> But it is by the prayers of the righteous that ye are spared;
> now therefore, if ye will cast out the righteous from among
> you then will not the Lord stay his hand; but in his fierce
> anger he will come out against you. (Alma 10:22–23.)

The prayers and the presence of the righteous hold back the
winds of destruction for Ammonihah. When the righteous are
destroyed the winds blow, and Ammonihah falls in war in a
single day.

Samuel gives an identical warning to the city of Zarahemla
prior to the Savior's birth: "When ye shall cast out the righteous from among you," he cries from the wall, "then shall ye
be ripe for destruction" (Helaman 13:12–14). The Savior,
speaking through the darkness after the destruction, explains
the final cause of Zarahemla's downfall: "And because they
did cast them all out, that there were none righteous among
them, I did send down fire and destroy them" (3 Nephi 9:11).

The Old Testament also bears witness to these truths. In the
last days before Jerusalem's destruction by Babylon, the Lord
challenges Jeremiah to "run . . . to and fro through the streets
of Jerusalem, and see now, and know, and seek in the broad
places thereof, if ye can find a man, if there be any that executeth judgment, that seeketh the truth; and I will pardon it"
(Jeremiah 5:1). Later the Lord tells Ezekiel, "I sought for a man
among them, that should make up the hedge, and stand in the
gap before me for the land, that I should not destroy it: but I
found none" (Ezekiel 22:30).

Nephi, speaking of the Canaanites, tells his own rebellious
brothers the final cause of Canaanite destruction: "But behold,
this people had rejected every word of God, and they were ripe
in iniquity" (1 Nephi 17:35).

The casting out of the righteous, including the murder of

the prophets, is the last step on the road to a fulness of iniquity. Abraham prayed that the Lord would spare Sodom and Gomorrah if he could find ten righteous souls. He could find only three, Lot and his two daughters. These the Lord removed before the destruction. The removal of the righteous brings the same result as if the righteous were destroyed or cast out. The Lord will not always let the wicked destroy the righteous. He often spares them by leading them into the wilderness, as he did Lehi, Mosiah, Alma, and many other prophets and peoples. Isaiah states that "the righteous perisheth, and no man layeth it to heart: and merciful men are taken away, none considering that the righteous is taken away from the evil to come" (Isaiah 57:1).

Prophetic Warnings

Before they are killed, cast out, or removed by the Lord, the righteous and the prophets issue a warning. This warning is followed by either a reversal of the trends of wickedness, leading to repentance, or an acceleration of the corrupting forces, leading to the fulness of iniquity. Ammonihah is an excellent example of this principle. The scriptures record that between Alma's first and second warnings "the people did wax more gross in their iniquities" (Alma 8:28). This same principle is seen immediately after the warning cries of Samuel the Lamanite: "There was but little alteration in the affairs of the people [after his warning], save it were the people began to be more hardened in iniquity, and do more and more of that which was contrary to the commandments of God" (Helaman 16:12).

The Lord is patient; he will strive with man as long as possible. Therefore, a second, a third, and a fourth warning is often given. Each warning typically is stronger than the last. Second witnesses are sent, usually ones that strike a little closer to home. In Ammonihah the Lord provides the second witness. Ironically, the people request another witness by challenging Alma to produce one: "Suppose ye that we shall believe the testimony of one man?" (Alma 9:2.) The second witness is Amulek.

Amulek, being a citizen of Ammonihah and "a man of no small reputation" (Alma 10:4), testifies of the wickedness among them, which he knows by his own experience. His ability to converse with and finally defeat the trickery of their foremost lawyer, Zeezrom, provides the people with ample evidence that they should repent. But his testimony converts only Zeezrom and a few others. The majority harden their hearts even more.

The Lord then provides the people of Ammonihah with a third warning and a third witness. Once again his witness is well chosen: Zeezrom, their former champion, becomes their accuser. (A close parallel to this is seen just before the Jewish destruction of A.D. 70, with the Apostle Paul serving as a "Zeezrom" to the Jews.) The people by now have heard enough and refuse to listen. They stone Zeezrom and chase him and others out of the city; then they burn the believers' wives and children in a mockery of the burning fires of hell. A final witness is sent—the Lord's own. An earthquake destroys the lawyers and judges who have imprisoned Alma and Amulek and who ordered the burning of the women and children.

The Lord indicates that the witness of the force of nature will also be given before the Second Coming: "After your testimony cometh wrath and indignation upon the people. For after your testimony cometh the testimony of earthquakes, that shall cause groanings in the midst of her, and men shall fall upon the ground and shall not be able to stand." (D&C 88:88–89.)

Alma and Amulek leave Ammonihah after the earthquake. Even this final testimony has no effect on the citizens of Ammonihah. "They yet remained a hard-hearted and a stiff-necked people; and they repented not of their sins, ascribing all the power of Alma and Amulek to the devil; for they were of the profession of Nehor, and did not believe in the repentance of their sins" (Alma 15:15).

Refusal to Repent

The last phrase of the above scripture is a crucial one; it describes a common attitude of a "fulness" people. They "wilfully rebel" (3 Nephi 6:18; 4 Nephi 1:38), having no intention of repenting of their sins no matter how miserable they become as a result of them. They do not believe in repentance, rationalizing all behavior and justifying disobedience to laws and values. Like the Jaredites and the Nephites in their futile last struggles, they would rather die than repent. At this point it becomes clear that the Lord will "not always suffer them to take happiness in sin" (Mormon 2:13). His Spirit "shall not always strive with man" (Genesis 6:3; Moses 8:17). When detailing the destruction of his people, Mormon emphasizes on numerous occasions the refusal of the people to repent. (See Mormon 2:8,13; 3:2–3,13,15; 4:10; 5:2,11; 6:17.)

The refusal to repent in the face of destruction is dramatically portrayed in Amos's repetition of the phrase, "Yet have ye not returned unto me, saith the Lord" (Amos 4:6, 8–10). This phrase is repeated after five verses that detail the sufferings of Israel's wicked inhabitants. That same refusal in the face of misery is envisioned by John in Revelation as he looks at the last days. He too repeats the phrase, "and they repented not" (Revelation 16:9, 11; 9:21). The ultimate "casting out" of righteousness is the rejection of repentance—the only principle that can reverse the downward spiral.

The people assume one of two destructive attitudes that lock out any hope for an eventual turning of their hearts back to God. Isaiah painted a powerful picture of one of these attitudes when speaking of Israel. "In that day did the Lord God of Hosts call to weeping, and to mourning, and to baldness, and to girding with sackcloth." These are all activities associated with repentance. However, the people rejected the Lord's call and had one last fling before the day of destruction. "And behold joy and gladness, [revelry], slaying oxen, and killing sheep, eating flesh, and drinking wine: Let us eat and drink; for tomorrow we shall die." (Isaiah 22:12–13.) The oft-quoted phrase "Eat, drink, and be merry" has specific associations to the final activities of a fulness people. There is no thought of a change of behavior, only a last wild party.

Against the backdrop of this complacent attitude is that of

"curse God and die." When Mormon saw the sorrow of his people during the last great battles of destruction, he had some hope that they would now repent. "But this my joy was vain, for their sorrowing was not unto repentance. . . . And they did not come unto Jesus with broken hearts and contrite spirits, but they did curse God, and wish to die. Nevertheless they would struggle with the sword for their lives." (Mormon 2:13–14.) Given the choice between "Look to God and live" (Alma 37:47), "Eat, drink and be merry," and "Curse God and die," they willfully choose destruction.

The Fulness of God's Wrath

Another phrase is usually associated with the fulness of iniquity and the refusal to repent: "the fulness of God's wrath." The fulness of God's wrath is not always seen in a fiery destruction. It is also manifested by withdrawal of his Spirit. The withdrawal comes at the point when the Lord says: "I can do nothing more for you. You have rejected every effort I have made to redeem you. Therefore, I leave you to yourself to suffer the full impact of your sins. If you will not change, they will bring you to destruction." Has not a father's anger reached its fullest proportion when he gives up on his children and leaves them to learn for themselves the hard lessons and consequences of wrong choices?

How many times did the Lord try to turn Laman and Lemuel around with dreams, a father's and a brother's exhortations, his own voice, angels, storms, and shocks? But they would not listen. He then left them to their own spiritual darkness. "In vain have I smitten your children," the Lord laments through Jeremiah; "they received no correction: your own sword hath devoured your prophets, like a destroying lion" (Jeremiah 2:30). The Lord tells Ezekiel, "I have consumed them with the fire of my wrath: their own way have I recompensed upon their heads" (Ezekiel 22:31). A generation before Ezekiel it was revealed to Isaiah that Israel's "iniquity shall not be purged from you till ye die" (Isaiah 22:14). Micah tells his rebellious listeners, "For her wound is incurable" (Micah 1:9). And yet the Lord continues to warn. In the first verses of Jeremiah 1 we learn that Jeremiah's words came "unto the carrying away of Jerusalem captive" (Jeremiah 1:3). In spite of the people's rebellion, the prophets, with charity and anxiety, continue to testify until it is too late. The tragedy is that the destruction is preventable if the people will only take their medicine. "Is there no balm in Gilead;" Jeremiah laments, "is there no physician there? Why then is not the health of the daughter of my people recovered?" (Jeremiah 8:22).

The Prayers of the Righteous

When the fulness is nearing, the prophets, despite all their charity and concern, often cannot pray for the doomed civilization. Amulek said it was not only the presence of the righteous but their prayers that saved Ammonihah. Abraham bargained with the Lord to save Sodom and Gomorrah for the righteous who were there, until even he could not go below ten righteous people. Mormon informed Moroni, "I cannot recommend them unto God lest he should smite me" (Moroni 9:21). When he earlier had endeavored to preach to his people, he found that his "mouth was shut, and I was forbidden" (Mormon 1:16). We read in Moses 8:25 that "it repented Noah, and his heart was pained that the Lord had made man on the earth." Before the Babylonian captivity the Lord tells Jeremiah, "Therefore pray not thou for this people, neither lift up cry nor prayer for them, neither make intercession to me: for I will not hear thee" (Jeremiah 7:16).

This command occurs again in Jeremiah 11:14 and 14:11. It is a dark day when the love of a Mormon or a Noah must be restrained because the people are not worthy of their petitions. The prayers of the righteous cease as the fulness of iniquity overflows.

6

REJECTION OF VALUES AND ABSOLUTES

I T WAS POINTED OUT EARLIER that the casting out of the righteous represents both the beginning and the end of the fulness of iniquity. The rejection of the righteous involves more than rejecting people or stoning prophets; it encompasses the rejection of principles, commandments, values, and ethics. A fulness-of-iniquity society fights to destroy the very laws and morals that inspire the righteous.

Isaiah linked the destruction of the Israelites to this rejection. "Therefore, as the fire devoureth the stubble, and the flame consumeth the chaff, so their root shall be as rotteness, and their blossom go up as dust: because they have cast away the law of the Lord of hosts, and despised the word of the Holy One of Israel" (Isaiah 5:24). Isaiah's images of dryness in the above passage suggest a people devoid of any spiritual values. Regardless of advancements in technology, medicine, communication, and so forth, when a society rejects the Ten Commandments and the Sermon on the Mount they are not progressing. They live under the false illusion of moving forward, but their movement is towards disintegration, not greater civilization. It is a sad commentary when "Thou shalt not commit adultery" and other straightforward counsels have numerous amendments attached to them.

The Casting Out of the Righteous

In this situation an attitude of mockery and cynicism

develops. Samuel warned Zarahemla, "Ye do cast out the prophets, and *do mock them*" (Helaman 13:24; italics added). Jacob gave a similar warning to his people by asking them several questions. "Will ye reject the words of the prophets . . . and deny the good word of Christ, and the power of God . . . and quench the Holy Spirit, and make a mock of the great plan of salvation?" (Jacob 6:8.)

The people of Ammonihah burned the scriptures, but before that symbolic act they had rejected the teachings of the scriptures. Casting out the righteous begins with the mockery of good and the elimination of traditional, eternal, absolute values. The declining Israelite people reversed their value systems, causing Isaiah to cry, "Woe unto them that call evil good, and good evil; that put darkness for light, and light for darkness; that put bitter for sweet, and sweet for bitter!" (Isaiah 5:20.) A curse was prophesied for the earth because it was "defiled under the inhabitants thereof," they having "transgressed the laws, changed the ordinance, broken the everlasting covenant" (Isaiah 24:5).

Jeremiah tells the inhabitants of Jerusalem, "Ye have perverted the words of the living God" (Jeremiah 23:36). This was nothing new. They had been changing the laws of righteousness from the beginning. Amos attributed their errors to "their lies," warning that the Lord would "not turn away the punishment thereof; because they [had] despised the law of the Lord, and [had] not kept his commandments" (Amos 2:4).

Amulek condemns the lawyers of Ammonihah because they are "laying plans to pervert the ways of the righteous, and to bring down the wrath of God upon your heads, even to the utter destruction of this people" (Alma 10:18). He refers to the warning given by Mosiah at the time when the government leadership was changed from kings to elected judges: "Well did he say that if the time should come that the voice of this people should choose iniquity, . . . they would be ripe for destruction" (Alma 10:19). Amulek then tells the citizens of Ammonihah that "the foundation of the destruction of this people is beginning to be laid by the unrighteousness of your lawyers and your judges" (Alma 10:27). What motivated these lawyers to pervert laws? In true "fulness" fashion, their object was "to get gain" (Alma 10:32).

During another period of Nephite history, the laws were being corrupted by the authorities of the land who laid "aside the commandments of God . . . doing no justice unto the children of men." The laws were changed "that they might the more easily commit adultery, and steal, and kill, and do according to their own wills." (Helaman 7:4–5.) Generally speaking, laws that rest upon a foundation of "the commandments of God" (Mosiah 29:11,13,25) are best calculated to insure the peace, stability and happiness of a community. Those that "more easily" allow one to disregard those commandments, in time, will produce just the opposite. The constant looking for legal loopholes with an emphasis on winning cases or legislative battles without a true regard for justice becomes the ambition of the day. The Lord blessed the Nephites with a free form of government based on law much as he has us today, but they misused the gift. The Lord "looked for judgment," Isaiah said, "but behold oppression; for righteousness, but behold a cry" (Isaiah 5:7).

However, it was not only the lawyers, judges, and government officials that led the people to destruction; the people chose it themselves by their rejection of eternal values and truths. It was the people who defended their own and their lawyers' wickedness against the charges of the prophets. Ammonihah's citizens are reminiscent of Noah's kingdom, where the people burned Abinadi after claiming to be "guiltless" (Mosiah 12:14).

The lawyers of Amulek's time were no different than the forces of evil during the final days of the Nephites. Mormon wrote to his son Moroni that the people were "seeking to put down all power and authority which cometh from God . . . and after rejecting so great a knowledge, my son, they must perish soon" (Moroni 8:28–29). Undoubtedly much of this attempt was done through the formal legal systems of the day and the twisted interpretation of Nephite laws.

History has shown that there is a natural pattern of decline in societies. First, spiritual values are fought and destroyed. Since religious-spiritual truths are the only force strong enough to maintain moral behavior in a civilization, morality and ethics decline next. With the decline of morality, culture and civilization dies. It is often suggested by the opponents of spiritual truth that a people can flourish in a moral society devoid of religious convictions, but history has proven otherwise. No people have been able to create a moral climate independent of a religious base. The scriptures especially testify to this truth.

Criticism and the Charge of "Bondage"

The major influences we have examined up to this point hinge on the "turning of things upside down." Beliefs, values, and behaviors are eliminated by subtle mockery, epitomized by Korihor. He, like all anti-Christs, used two of Satan's most effective tools—cynical, sophisticated criticism and the charge of "bondage." Both are very effective in eliminating the eternal values of right and wrong.

The first tool is apparent in the words and phrases spoken by Korihor. He accuses the Nephites of having "a *foolish* and vain hope," of following "*foolish traditions* of [their] fathers." Their belief "is the effect of a *frenzied mind;* and this *derangement* of [their] minds comes because of the traditions of [their] fathers." They are deceived by "*foolish* ordinances . . . laid down by ancient priests"; their values and commandments are nothing but "*traditions* and . . . *dreams* and . . . *whims* and . . . *visions,*" all of which are "*silly.*" (Alma 30:13, 14, 23, 28, 31; italics added.) All these phrases exhibit the clever sophistication often seen in the modern world, a sophistication that seeks to replace traditional beliefs and values because they are old or outdated, and speaks of "new moralities." In our own society such words as *puritanical* or *victorian* suggest the same sophisticated mockery of traditional morality.

The second tool is best understood in the subtle suggestion

Satan used against Eve when he asked, "Yea, hath God said— *Ye shall not* eat of every tree of the garden?" (Moses 4:7; italics added.) Satan wanted Eve to believe that commandments were threats to her agency. Korihor uses the same technique: "O ye that are bound down, . . . why do ye yoke yourselves?" he cries. "I do not teach this people to bind themselves down under the foolish ordinances and performances which are laid down . . . to usurp power and authority over them"; "I say they are in bondage"; "they durst not enjoy their rights and privileges." (Alma 30:13, 23, 24, 27.)

Those who believe these words take pride in sin. The followers of Korihor "lift up their heads in wickedness, yea, leading away many women, and also men, to commit whoredoms" (Alma 30:18). The immorality discussed earlier is often the result of people's believing that morality "binds them down."

All Things Become Relative

Into the vacuum left by the mocked eternal absolutes creep the beginnings of the fulness of iniquity. Everything becomes "relative" and "subjective." Old values and absolutes— branded as "foolish traditions," the "effects of frenzied minds," or "derangements"—are discarded. Judgments cannot be passed on behavior, because there is no eternal standard of right and wrong to which one can appeal. People do not see truths, ethics, and morality as eternal and unchanging. Instead they match their values to their inordinate goals and desires. As Korihor expounded, "Whatsoever a man did was no crime" (Alma 30:17). Thus "righteousness" is cast out. The only guide that can keep man from his natural self is eliminated. Eventually he becomes "an enemy to God and to all righteousness."

Ample evidence of this fact exists in today's society. Time-honored ideals—once firmly believed by Western man—are challenged: Beauty, Truth, and Goodness are eroded, challenged by constant redefinition and relativity. Judgments of wrong or unrighteous behavior become more and more rare. Popular philosophy denies absolutes. This leads to the rejection of God's standards as universal for all people at all times.

When a society changes the old verities, giving license to immoral life-styles by claiming they are "new" or "liberating" or "modern," the downward spiral accelerates. Remember, first true religion dies, then morality, and finally civilization.

No Accountability For Sin

Linked to these false assertions is an unwillingness to accept responsibility for one's sins. When Mosiah changed the government from kings to judges, one of his reasons was to make men accountable for their actions. Though the people were grateful that "every man [could] enjoy his rights and privileges," each man also "expressed a willingness to answer for his own sins" (Mosiah 29:30). Rights and privileges must always be balanced with responsibility. When explaining to Joseph Smith the purpose of the Constitution, the Lord repeated Mosiah's teachings. One of the major functions of the Constitution was to give man "moral agency;" which meant "every man may be accountable for his own sins in the day of judgment" (D&C 101:78). The Lord warned if there is "more or less" than this balance "it cometh of evil" (D&C 98:7). In today's society we hear the incessant drumbeat of "more" rights, inevitably accompanied by the desire for "less" accountability. There is always someone else to blame in a world where "spin" takes the place of excuseless acknowledgement of wrong. Pornography, abortion, homosexuality, hatred, and so forth, are presented as issues of rights and privileges, not morality, until more and more the Constitution is used as a rationalization to commit sin in the name of freedom instead of being used as it was intended by the Lord—to make people accountable for their sins. Perhaps this trend will give us insight into the reasons why the Constitution will hang by a thread.

The False Indignation of a "Fulness" People

Ironically, the "fulness" societies claim to be just and righteous; they take offense in the suggestion that they are otherwise. Nehor defended his perversion and murder "with much boldness" (Alma 1:11). Korihor spoke against Alma "in great swelling words," accusing him of restricting the people from "enjoying their rights and privileges" (Alma 30:27, 31). The righteous, who decry the society's perversions as evil, are condemned by the people as evil themselves, for the "sin" of intolerance toward new or changing life-styles. In Ammonihah "they cried out, saying: This man doth revile against our laws which are just, and our wise lawyers whom we have selected" (Alma 10:24). Noah's people, with indignation and offense, assured their puppet king, "Behold, we are guiltless, and thou, O king, hast not sinned" (Mosiah 12:14). Aaron's missionary labors brought him face to face with the Amalekites, who accused him of bigotry, superiority, and intolerance by saying: "Behold are not this people as good as thy people? Thou also sayest, except we repent we shall perish. How knowest thou the thoughts and intent of our hearts? How knowest thou that we have cause to repent? How knowest thou that we are not a righteous people?" (Alma 21:5–6.)

Micah shows us this behavior as it existed among the Israelites, particularly among those who claimed to be the most religious. They "judge for reward, and the priests thereof teach for hire, and the prophets thereof divine for money: yet will they lean upon the Lord, and say, Is not the Lord among us? none evil can come upon us. Therefore shall Zion for your sake be plowed as a field, and Jerusalem shall become heaps." (Micah 3:11–12.)

The Lord's warning to Cain, before he formed the first secret combination and murdered his brother Abel, contained an explanation of what happens when righteousness is "cast out":

If thou doest well, thou shalt be accepted. And if thou doest not well, sin lieth at the door, and Satan desireth to have thee; and except thou shalt hearken unto my commandments, I will deliver thee up, and it shall be unto thee according to his desire. (Moses 5:23.)

Ceasing to "do well" opens the door to "sin," which is patiently waiting to enter. Clearly the Lord would have his people fill their lives so full of "good" that there will be no room for evil when it knocks. Slowly casting out the righteous by not "doing well" may be what the Lord means when he says over and over again that the people "dwindle" in unbelief.

Sinning Against the Greater Light

There is a correlation between the fulness of iniquity and the amount of light that is sinned against. As John Steinbeck wrote in *The Winter of Our Discontent*, "It's so much darker when a light goes out than it would have been if it had never shone" ([New York: Viking Press, 1961], p. 281). In most cases it is the blessed, enlightened societies that reach the fulness of iniquity and are destroyed. "He who sins against the greater light shall receive the greater condemnation" (D&C 82:3). Amulek expressed this relationship clearly to the people of Ammonihah:

> And now behold I say unto you, that if this people, who have received so many blessings from the hand of the Lord, should transgress contrary to the light and knowledge which they do have, I say unto you that if this be the case, that if they should fall into transgression, it would be far more tolerable for the Lamanites than for them (Alma 9:23).

These thoughts echo the words of the dying Lehi to his sons. Lehi prophesied: "When the time cometh that they shall dwindle in unbelief, after they have received so great blessings from the hand of the Lord . . . behold, the judgments of him that is just shall rest upon them. . . . He will cause them to be scattered and smitten." (2 Nephi 1:10–11.) When Alma gave his parting testimony to his son Helaman, he prophesied the destruction of the Nephites in the fourth generation after the visit of the Savior. While speaking of the Nephite "works of darkness, and lasciviousness," Alma said that the wicked would be destroyed "because they shall sin against so great light and knowledge" (Alma 45:12). Nephi the Second warned his generation "that it shall be better for the Lamanites than for you except ye shall repent. . . .They have not sinned against that great knowledge which ye have received." (Helaman 7:23–24.)

In both Alma 9 and 2 Nephi 1, the prophets are specific in naming the "light," or the blessings and knowledge, that would be sinned against. The following blessings should be familiar to modern society, for they are the blessings America has received throughout its history. The following lists come directly from the scriptures:

2 Nephi 1:10
1. "Having a knowledge of the creation of the earth, and all men."
2. "Knowing the great and marvelous works of the Lord from the creation."
3. "Having power given them to do all things by faith."
4. "Having all the commandments from the beginning."
5. "Having been brought by his infinite goodness into this precious land of promise."
6. Knowing "the Holy One of Israel, the true Messiah, their Redeemer and their God."

A dwindling people begin to reject these blessings. They lose the belief in the creation of man by a wise Creator, substituting it with alternate theories; lose a knowledge of the stories and truths of the scriptures; lose the faith in God that enables them to accomplish noble works such as the founding of this nation or the pioneer sacrifices of our ancestors; lose an understanding of the need to maintain society by obedience to the commandments; fail to express gratitude for the opportunities and advantages of living in a blessed land while they demand more and more. Rejecting Christ does not only consist in an open defiance of his divinity; rather, as Nephi states, "they set him at naught, and hearken not to the voice of his counsels" (I Nephi 19:7). Alma gave a similar list of the gifts of God to a people favored to live on a promised land.

Alma 9:20–22
1. "Having been favored above every other nation, kindred, tongue, or people."
2. "Having had all things made known unto them, according to their desires, and their faith, and prayers."
3. "Having been visited by the Spirit of God."
4. "Having been spoken unto by the voice of the Lord."
5. "Having the spirit of prophecy, and the spirit of revelation."
6. "And also many gifts . . . and the gift of the Holy Ghost."
7. "Having been delivered of God."
8. "Having been saved from famine, and from sickness, and all manner of diseases."
9. "Having waxed strong in battle."
10. "Having been brought out of bondage . . . and preserved."
11. "Hav[ing] been prospered until they are rich in all manner of things."

The blessings of Alma's list as they relate to modern society are self-explanatory. Clearly it is the favored, chosen, promised, or elect peoples who are in the greatest danger of "dwindling" into a fulness of iniquity. In the last wars of the Nephites and Lamanites, the Lamanites were "brutal" and "without civilization." We read, for example, that they sacrificed women and children to idol gods. But it was the Nephites who suffered destruction. Having "sin[ned] against the greater light," they "receive[d] the greater condemnation" (D&C 82:3).

7

WARNINGS TO A
MODERN WORLD

IS THERE A PURPOSE IN STIRRING UP the ashes of fallen societies? Are not such things better left alone? Certainly the scriptures offer more positive, uplifting topics to examine. But in those ashes one finds a touchstone for all civilizations, both those described in scripture and others. A study of this type proves valuable when it is applied. Moroni, the author who so conscientiously warned today's Gentiles again and again, teaches the need to understand the fulness of iniquity:

> Behold, I speak unto you as though I spake from the dead; for I know that ye shall have my words.
> Condemn me not because of mine imperfection, neither my father, because of his imperfection, neither them who have written before him; but rather give thanks unto God that he hath made manifest unto you our imperfections, that ye may learn to be more wise than we have been. (Mormon 9:30–31.)

Moroni hoped the "Gentiles" would not "continue" in their sins until the fulness came (Ether 2:11). Modern man lives in a society where a magnitude of problems confronts him daily. Often solutions to these problems create even greater challenges. The Savior prophesied of a day when there would be "upon the earth distress of nations, with perplexity" (Luke 21:25). Man speaks of the threat of nuclear war with its attendant nuclear winter. He is concerned with the international jousting of the superpowers and polarizes himself behind economic theories, political ideologies, and national identities. Those who differ are viewed as enemies. Latter-day Saints study the signs of the times and look for clues. Perhaps it is time to stop the shouting and look inward, to cleanse the "inward vessel" and then concentrate on the "outer vessel" (Alma 60:23).

The Inner Enemy

Are the greatest enemies those from without or those from within? Usually the greatest concern is directed to those from without. People concentrate on fighting and preparing for "outer vessel" enemies. Yet often the inner enemy has a more dire effect.

Could the scriptures have provided a more complete list than they do of the major societal problems in America, and indeed in the West? The Lord's promise to the Americas is that they need not fear any "outer vessel" as long as the inner one is kept in order. The increase in pornography, organized crime, gangs, political scandals, drug abuse, abortion, wife and child abuse, children killing children, hard rock music and MTV (and their fascination with evil), militarism, materialism, and violence are not difficult to see in today's society. Even among Latter-day Saints the influences of the world are seen.

Entertained by Iniquity

Perhaps one of the most critical observations one could make against modern society is that people are "entertained" by the numerous aspects of the fulness of iniquity. Movies, literature, television, music, and other forms of entertainment are often an outpouring of violence, immorality, victimization of women and children, crime, the occult, the power plays of money in high society, the mockery of traditional values, and the glorification of war. Edith Hamilton, a noted author on the Greek and Roman civilizations, remarked: "There is no better indication of what the people of any period are like than the plays they go to see. Popular drama shows the public quality as nothing else can." (*The Roman Way* [New York: Avon Books, 1960].) As Latter-day Saints let us not contribute to the problem by our patronage of entertainment that has as its focus the fulness of iniquity. For example, we have been requested many times by the prophets and Apostles to not attend R-rated movies. Our own standard of entertainment is clearly outlined in the 1990 Church booklet *For the Strength of Youth.* "Don't attend or participate in any form of entertainment, including concerts, movies, and video cassettes, that is vulgar, immoral, inappropriate, suggestive, or pornographic in any way. Movie ratings do not always accurately reflect offensive content." (P. 12.)

Prophecies of a Latter-day Fulness

Prophecies concerning the last days speak of a time of "wickedness and vengeance" (Moses 7:60) that will lead to another major destruction of the wicked at the Savior's second coming. A cursory study of the latter-day prophecies reveals the same iniquities of society preceding the "great day of the Lord" that brought down ancient peoples. The insights gleaned from the scriptures give a valuable societal "sign" that hits closer to home than famines, earthquakes, plagues, and darkened suns or moons.

John described Satan's kingdom in the last days as a seven-headed beast. This image fits all times. Satan's kingdom is patterned after its maker, who is depicted as a seven-headed dragon. In the book of Revelation the wound in one of the heads healed, hydra-like. This is a fitting symbol of Satan's ever-growing influence. The destruction of one form of evil or the elimination of one head is most often followed by new evils. It would be foolish indeed to single out one head and proclaim, "voilà l'ennemi." Satan's kingdom has many heads and many horns in the last days. Latter-day Saints must be aware of them all, lest they find themselves fighting a crusade against one head while the others continue unheeded.

The Latter-day Saints and Modern Babylon

In light of this, where do Latter-day Saints stand, and what is their responsibility? Again the scriptures are clear. They proclaim that God's "elect" must do two basic things. First, as might be expected, the Lord commands that they leave Babylon, for "I will not spare any that remain in Babylon" (D&C 64:24). The Latter-day Saints must not allow themselves to be compromised in any degree by the influences of the world that lead to the fulness of iniquity.

In light of the Lord's commandment to leave Babylon, we may find it useful to reflect on the story of Lot, told in Genesis. When the herdsmen of Lot and Abraham quarreled about the use of land after their entry into Canaan, Abraham, in a gesture of peace, allowed Lot the choice of whatever land he wanted. Lot "chose him all the plain of Jordan." Lot first pitched his tent in the plain that was "toward Sodom." The verse immediately following is interesting and could serve as a commentary on Lot's choice: "But the men of Sodom were wicked and sinners before the Lord exceedingly" (Genesis 13:13).

If Lot was aware of this at the time, what wisdom did he exercise in choosing to dwell in such close proximity to the great evil of Sodom? In the very next chapter (Genesis 14) Lot, "who dwelt in Sodom," is captured with the rest of the Sodomites by aggressive kings. Abraham rescues him and the king of Sodom, who offers him rewards. Abraham's attitude, shown by his response, carries a great truth and can be contrasted with Lot's choice to dwell with the Sodomites: "I have lift up mine hand unto the Lord, the most high God, the possessor of heaven and earth, that I will not take from a thread even to a shoelatchet, and that I will not take any thing that is thine, lest thou shouldest say, I have made Abram rich" (Genesis 14:22–23).

Abraham wanted nothing to do with Sodom, not even a shoelace's worth. He had decided to shun the evils of the world. The lesson of Lot is carried to its conclusion when Lot tries to persuade his sons-in-law to take their families from

Sodom, "but he seemed as one that mocked unto his sons in law" (Genesis 19:14). Lot loses members of his family in the destruction of Sodom, including his wife, whose desire to return brought her death. Even the two daughters who left with him showed by their subsequent actions that they may have been influenced by the sins of Sodom. Lot's family clearly demonstrates the folly and danger of the righteous, but perhaps unwise, "dwelling in Sodom."

Tasting the Goodness of Jesus

When I was a boy I worked on a ranch in northern Nevada. The one job I hated most was fixing fence. Holes in the fence were made by the cattle when they pushed against it trying to eat the grass on the other side. It didn't matter where the fence was placed, the cows always felt there was better grass outside its limits. They would stick their heads through the wires and push against them, eventually creating holes. They would even stretch out their long tongues as far as they could and lick the blades of grass into their mouths.

The Lord has set some fairly safe standards to protect his children. There is plenty of good green grass in the middle of the meadow. We are encouraged to seek after the lovely, virtuous, praiseworthy, and things of good report. Indeed, this is one of the safeguards against a grass-licking tendency. Mormon gave us one of the secrets of his own survival in a fulness world when he said: "I was visited of the Lord, and tasted and knew of the goodness of Jesus" (Mormon 1:15). This he did in his youth.

Tasting the good allows us to discriminate more carefully when the world offers alternative sweets. Often, however, we longingly look through the Lord's protecting fence to the entertainments, pleasures, ambitions, and desires of the world. We don't actually break out of the fence, but we poke our heads through the wires to lick the grass of the world. When we do this there is a very real danger that we will destroy our ability to taste the joys of the good, the true, and the beautiful.

Using another analogy, if we hear shouting too much, it eventually destroys our ability to hear a whisper, and the world knows little more than shouting.

I also noticed that more often than not the cows did not go through the holes they had created in the fence, but the calves did. As parents we must be careful that our pushing of the limits, counsels, and standards of the Church don't create the holes that our children will slip through. Our exceptions to the standards of the Church often become the norm for our children as spiritual erosion has its way.

"Labor in the Vineyard"

The scriptures tell us that the second major thing we must do is preach the gospel and seek to establish Zion. To counter the fulness of iniquity, the Lord has sent in the last days the *fulness of his gospel*. In his preface to the Doctrine and Covenants, the Lord explains that Babylon will fall, as all Babylons of the past have fallen. Then he adds, "Wherefore, I the Lord, knowing the calamity which should come upon the inhabitants of the earth, called upon my servant Joseph Smith, Jun., and spake unto him from heaven, and gave him commandments" (D&C 1:17). Here we encounter a force that can offset the seeds of destruction—the fulness of the gospel, lived and shared by the righteous. The Latter-day Saints must strive to be the ten in Sodom and Gomorrah, the Amuleks of Ammonihah, the Mormons and Moronis and Noahs. Though our labors may be no more successful than those of the prophets of old, the charge to the Church is clear: preach the gospel and gather the elect.

This labor is not only a response to the world and its only hope, but also a defense for us. The very preaching of the gospel protects one against the influence of the world. Elie Wiesel tells the story of a man who travels to Sodom to warn its inhabitants of their need to repent. He does all he can to get their attention without any success. Finally a child points out to him that all his efforts are useless, the people simply won't change. The man replies that he realized long ago that they were not listening. He then explains that he cried against their excesses at first because he believed he could change the people, but now he cries because he is afraid if he stops they will change him. The gospel has no room for gloom-and-doom prophets. The Lord is not negative. When he speaks of the last days, he always accompanies his predictions and warnings with two thoughts: First, he declares that "the righteous need not fear" (1 Nephi 22:17, 22). "See that ye be not troubled" (Joseph Smith—Matthew 1:23), Christ told his disciples, for "my disciples shall stand in holy places, and shall not be moved" (D&C 45:32). Second, the Lord gives a charge to his Saints to *do* something, the only thing that will permanently solve the problems—preach the gospel. Those who speak of the last days to instill fear or doom or to be sensationalistic do not have the Spirit of the Lord. Latter-day Saints must be positive. President Gordon B. Hinckley has said:

> Do not partake of the spirit so rife in our times. Look for good and build on it. There is so much of the strong and the decent and the beautiful to build upon. You are partakers of the gospel of Jesus Christ. The gospel means "good news." The message of the Lord is one of hope and salvation. The voice of the Lord is a voice of glad tidings. The work of the Lord is a work of glorious accomplishment. (Address given at BYU—Hawaii Campus, 18 June 1983.)

At the end of a period of war and destruction among the Nephites, Mormon gave the answer to the Latter-day Saints. It was an answer for his own times. It is an answer for all times. The conditions of the fifteen years he speaks about would fit almost any period of history. It certainly fits the last days:

> And from the first year to the fifteenth has brought to pass the destruction of many thousands of lives; yea, it has brought to pass an awful scene of bloodshed.
> And the bodies of many thousands are laid low in the earth, while the bodies of many thousands are moldering in heaps upon the face of the earth. . . .

And thus we see how great the inequality of man is because of sin and transgression, and the power of the devil, which comes by the cunning plans which he hath devised to ensnare the hearts of men.

And thus we see the great call of diligence of men to labor in the vineyards of the Lord. (Alma 28:10–14.)

The call to "labor in the vineyard" is a call to every Latter-day Saint. The Doctrine and Covenants echoes this mandate in connection with the destructions prophesied for the last days:

Behold, verily, verily, I say unto you, that the people in Ohio call upon me in much faith, thinking I will stay my hand in judgment upon the nations, but I cannot deny my word.

Wherefore lay to with your might and call faithful laborers into my vineyard, that it may be pruned for the last time.

And inasmuch as they do repent and receive the fulness of my gospel, and become sanctified, I will stay mine hand in judgment. (D&C 39:16–18.)

Again, the call to spread the gospel and gather the elect is the answer to the coming destruction.

In the allegory of the tame and wild olive trees, the Lord instructs his servant to bring other servants, "and they were few." The Lord commands the "few" to "go to, and labor in the vineyard, with your might. For behold, this is the last time that I shall nourish my vineyard; for the end is nigh at hand, and the season speedily cometh." (Jacob 5:70–71.) This last great pruning of the vineyard is the reason why Joseph Smith was called, as noted in the first section of the Doctrine and Covenants.

In a later section the Lord issues the following powerful plea and testimony: "O, ye nations of the earth, how often would I have gathered you together as a hen gathereth her chickens under her wings, but ye would not!" (D&C 43:24.) The Lord then gives a list of the numerous testimonies and calls he has issued. That list includes "the mouth of my ser-

vants, . . . angels, . . . by mine own voice, . . . voice of thunder-
ings, . . . lightnings, . . . tempests, . . . earthquakes, . . . hail-
storms, . . . famines and pestilences, . . . the great sound of a
trump, . . . the voice of judgment, and . . . mercy, . . . and by the
voice of glory and honor and the riches of eternal life, and [I]
would have saved you with an everlasting salvation." With a
tone of resignation and sorrow the Lord concludes, "But ye
would not!" (D&C 43:25.) Therefore "the day has come, when
the cup of the wrath of mine indignation is full" (D&C 43:26).
The Lord then gives his Saints instructions on what to do about
the wickedness and stubbornness of man. "Wherefore, labor
ye, labor ye in my vineyard for the last time—for the last time
call upon the inhabitants of the earth" (D&C 43:28).

Willing Jonahs Needed

This, then, is the charge given to the Lord's elect as the
world slips or dwindles into the fulness of iniquity. Notice the
plea of the Prophet Joseph Smith in the dedicatory prayer for
the Kirtland Temple:

> Put upon thy servants the testimony of the covenant, . . .
> that thy people may not faint in the day of trouble.
> And whatsoever city thy servants shall enter, and the
> people of that city receive their testimony, let thy peace and
> thy salvation be upon that city; that they may gather out of
> that city the righteous, that they may come forth to Zion, or to
> her stakes, the places of thine appointment, with songs of
> everlasting joy;
> And until this be accomplished, let not thy judgments fall
> upon that city. (D&C 109:38–40.)

The Saints may not stop the judgments from descending on
the world, but the righteous can first be gathered out, protected, and instructed. John writes of this gathering in the book
of Revelation. An angel ascends from the east to delay four
assigned angels from destroying the earth until the sealing in

the foreheads of the righteous has been accomplished. We learn later that the seal is the name of the Father (see Revelation 7:1–8; 14:1; 21:4). It serves as a protection to the righteous against the winds of destruction much as the lamb's blood protected the children of Israel from "the destroyer" (Exodus 12:23). These righteous souls will be gathered into the Lord's temple, for it is in his house that the protecting seal is placed. In the dedicatory prayer of the Kirtland Temple Joseph Smith said: "We ask thee, holy Father, to establish the people that shall worship, and honorably hold a name and standing in this thy house, to all generations and for eternity; . . . that no combination of wickedness shall have power to rise up and prevail over thy people upon whom thy name shall be put in this house" (D&C 109:24–26).

Once having been gathered into the safety of Zion, the Saints will be instructed by living prophets and Apostles. While describing the desolations of the last days, Joseph Smith counseled the Saints to "make yourselves acquainted with those men who like Daniel pray three times a day toward the House of the Lord. Look to the presidency and receive instruction." (TPJS p. 161.) For those who do this the promises of the Lord are certain. "The gates of hell shall not prevail against you; yea, and the Lord God will disperse the powers of darkness from before you, and cause the heavens to shake for your good and his name's glory" (D&C 21:6).

The Saints must not be discouraged if the world rejects the Lord's testimonies. Mormon and Moroni preached, even though they could not "recommend [their people] unto God" (Moroni 9:21). Mormon encouraged his son to "labor diligently," even though it was a labor without hope, "for if we should cease to labor, we should be brought under condemnation" (Moroni 9:6). While abridging the Jaredite history, Moroni prayed that the Lord would give the Gentiles of our day charity, that they would accept the lessons learned in the Book of Mormon. The Lord replied, "If they have not charity it mattereth not unto thee, thou hast been faithful" (Ether 12:37). The Saints must be faithful to their responsibilities to leave

Babylon and to preach the fulness of the gospel, trusting in the Lord's protection. Like Noah, they must preach until the rain starts falling, or, as with Jeremiah, until the day of captivity.

While the wicked "lose heart and fear" because the ship of the world seems to be driven by those who have no clear idea of how to solve mankind's problems, the Latter-day Saints have a well-defined course. It is positive and true. Alma, Nephi the son of Helaman, and the four sons of Mosiah gave up righteous and good positions of influence and power to "bear down in pure testimony" because they saw it as the only alternative. Major portions of the Book of Mormon record their results. When the Ninevehs of the world are about to be destroyed, the Lord needs willing Jonahs. This will always be the charge of the Lord's people until the Ninevehs have seen the "stretched out hand of the Lord" and have rejected or accepted it:

> Woe be unto the Gentiles, saith the Lord God of Hosts! For notwithstanding I shall lengthen out mine arm unto them from day to day, they will deny me; nevertheless, I will be merciful unto them, saith the Lord God, if they will repent and come unto me; for mine arm is lengthened out all the day long, saith the Lord God of Hosts. (2 Nephi 28:32.)

8

THE FULNESS OF
LIGHT AND TRUTH

IHAVE DEVOTED CONSIDERABLE SPACE to the fulness of iniquity. I have detailed the depths societies reach when they "continue" in their sins, rejecting the warnings of the prophets. The fulness of the wrath of the Lord results when he leaves a wicked society to its own self-destruction. But another fulness is promised to those who walk uprightly before the Lord. *Continuing* in that walk brings a fulness of light and truth. The society built by those who seek this higher fulness is called Zion.

The Greater Portion of the Word

In Ammonihah the rejection of the prophets led to a deeper and deeper involvement in wickedness. There was no plateau, only a continuation of the downward spiral. What of those who heed the words of the prophets and live righteously? Instead of second and third prophetic warnings and exhortations, the righteous receive light and truth. Alma taught this principle clearly at Ammonihah—a very appropriate place to explain this fundamental law. Alma explained that prophets "are laid under a strict command" to impart the "mysteries of God" in accordance with the "heed and diligence" men give them. "And they that will harden their hearts, to them is given the lesser portion of the word until they know nothing concerning his mysteries; and then they are taken captive by the devil." But to him "that will not harden his heart, to him is given the greater portion of the word, until it is given unto him

to know the mysteries of God until he know them in full."
(Alma 12:9–11.)

A good illustration of this principle is found in Lehi's last
blessings to his sons. The exhortations to righteousness that
Laman and Lemuel receive can be contrasted with the doctri-
nal explanation of the Fall and the Atonement that Jacob
receives. The rebellious elder brothers are urged to repent,
while the righteous Jacob is given eternal truth. Obedience to
the words of the Lord opens up the opportunity to receive
more of the "mysteries" of God until fullness is achieved. The
Lord taught this principle to the early Saints. "Yea, blessed are
they . . . who have obeyed my gospel; for they shall receive for
their reward the good things of the earth. . . . And they shall
also be crowned with blessings from above, yea, and with
commandments not a few, and with revelations in their time—
they that are faithful and diligent before me." (D&C 59:3–4.)

Continuing in God

The Doctrine and Covenants confirms the truth established
by Alma. Section 50 tells us that "he that receiveth light, and
continueth in God, receiveth more light; and that light groweth
brighter and brighter until the perfect day" (D&C 50:24; italics
added). The word *continueth* used here can be contrasted with
Moroni's use of the word while speaking of the fulness of iniquity (see Ether 2:10–11). If one continues to follow the light or
obeys it, more light is received. That light grows until the "perfect day." Section 50 teaches that a man who is "ordained of
God" and follows the light can become a "possessor of all
things." The Lord continues: "But no man is possessor of all
things except he be purified and cleansed from all sin." (D&C
50:26–28.) Righteousness, obedience, and purification render
an individual worthy of receiving more light and truth.

Through Joseph Smith the Saints learned that "there is a
law, irrevocably decreed in heaven before the foundations of
this world, upon which all blessings are predicated—and

when we obtain any blessing from God, it is by obedience to that law upon which it is predicated" (D&C 130:20–21). What is the law upon which continued reception of light and truth is predicated? Is it not obedience to the light already given, and the allowing of that light, through the Atonement, to purify us and mold our characters so that we become Christlike? The Doctrine and Covenants further states that "no man receiveth a fulness unless he keepeth [God's] commandments. He that keepeth his commandments receiveth truth and light, until he is glorified in truth and knoweth all things." (D&C 93:27–28.)

The Lord also taught that the "wicked one cometh and taketh away light and truth, through disobedience" (D&C 93:39). Once again it is shown that obedience brings the "blessing" of light and truth, while disobedience causes the loss of it.

Intelligence, Light, Truth, Spirit

The words *light* and *truth* carry many meanings, and a full definition is difficult to formulate. However, many scriptural verses give insight by providing companion words. These help clarify exactly what one receives through obedience. "The glory of God is intelligence, or, in other words, light and truth," God told Joseph Smith (D&C 93:36). This verse, broken down into a formula, reads as follows:

Glory = Intelligence = Light and Truth

The terms are synonymous. Obedience, therefore, to light brings with it increased glory, intelligence, and truth. The list of synonyms can be expanded with additional scriptures. Section 84 teaches, "The word of the Lord is truth, and whatsoever is truth is light, and whatsoever is light is Spirit, even the Spirit of Jesus Christ" (D&C 84:45). The Savior affirms in section 88, "My voice is Spirit; my Spirit is truth" (D&C 88:66).

The expanded formula now reads:

Word of the Lord = Truth = Light = Glory = Intelligence = Spirit = Spirit of Jesus Christ

It is difficult to define intelligence, glory, light, truth, the Spirit of Jesus Christ, and like terms concretely. We can comprehend, however, that it is this light, this intelligence, that God the Father and his Son have a fulness of, and that they are therefore beings worthy of man's worship.

"Full of Grace and Truth"

The Father and the Son are commonly described as being "full of grace and truth" (2 Nephi 2:6). Alma uses this phrase several times. "I know that Jesus Christ shall come," he says, "yea, the Son, the Only Begotten of the Father, full of grace, and mercy, and truth" (Alma 5:48). Alma later gives a fuller description, stating that "the Only Begotten of the Father" is "full of grace, equity, and truth, full of patience, mercy, and long-suffering" (Alma 9:26; see also Alma 13:9; D&C 66:12).

In Doctrine and Covenants 93 we learn that Christ "received not of the fulness at first, but continued from grace to grace, until he received a fulness" (D&C 93:12–14). This truth is so important that the Lord repeated it three times in succession in the above verses. The Savior, advancing or *continuing* from one degree of light and truth to another, or from one degree of grace to another, received a "fulness." All mankind is then promised, "If you keep my commandments you shall receive of his fulness, and be glorified in me as I am in the Father; therefore, I say unto you, you shall receive grace for grace" (D&C 93:20). To continue from one degree of grace or light to another is to be constantly obedient; this is Christ's example. Thus "he received a fulness of truth, yea, even of all truth" (D&C 93:26). This is the path he invites all to follow.

The same relationship of obedience and light is taught in Doctrine and Covenants 88. It gives added insight on growing from grace to grace. The Lord first reveals that

> my voice is Spirit; my Spirit is truth; truth abideth and hath no end; and if it be in you it shall abound.

> And if your eye be single to my glory, your whole bodies shall be filled with light, and there shall be no darkness in you; and that body which is filled with light comprehendeth all things.
>
> Therefore, sanctify yourselves that your minds become single to God. (D&C 88:66–68.)

Here man is instructed to turn all his energies and desires to the will and light of the Lord. This is what it means to have an eye single to God's glory: man's will is swallowed up in the will of the Father. If an individual does this, light will abound, will chase darkness away, and will bring a comprehension of all things. Man is told to allow that light to sanctify him and to become single to God.

Alma taught the inhabitants of Ammonihah that those who accept the word of the Lord receive more of his words until they know all mysteries. The Doctrine and Covenants teaches that light, truth, and intelligence are given to those who continue in God, keep his commandments, are purified and cleansed from all sin, have an eye single to God's glory, and sanctify themselves. Those who "continue" in light and truth receive a promise that they can eventually have a fulness, as do the Father and the Son. The Savior progressed from grace to grace in this manner, thus setting the example.

Perfection and Godliness

The Father and the Son are described as being full of light and truth. They are also full of "grace, equity, . . . patience, mercy, and long-suffering" (Alma 9:26). Other traits could be listed, such as charity, justice, kindness, and meekness. A quick survey of these traits reveals that they are the exact opposite of those Mormon ascribed to his people when he said they were "without civilization," "without principle," "without mercy," and "without order." It is evident from the attributes of God that obedience to the commandments leads to the building of a certain type of character. That character includes all the traits of godliness. There is a direct correlation between a man's character and the amount of light and truth he receives. Obviously light, truth, and intelligence increase the attributes of godliness in any individual. The accompanying graph illustrates this relationship.

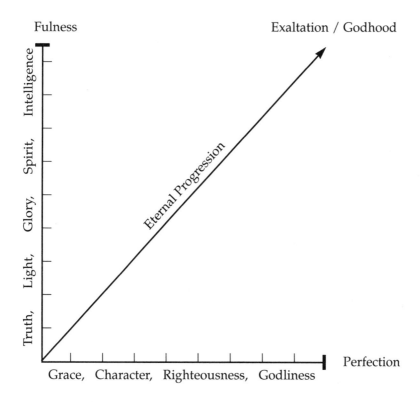

As people develop character by acquiring the attributes of godliness, they receive light, truth, and intelligence. These in turn help them improve and direct their character growth. Just as increased light in a disorderly room enables one to see more clearly the cobwebs and dust in the corners, so does increased spiritual light reveal the more minute areas of an individual's character that need refining. It is not necessarily a bad sign if one feels a constant need to repent and improve. It is an indication that he or she is responding to the light being given.

After acquiring all the attributes of God in perfection, man can receive a fulness of light and truth. Meantime the more he obeys, the more light and truth he is given; and the more light he receives, the more he can obey and progress. When perfection and godliness are achieved, one is full of light and truth, having "chased darkness away." One can then be exalted as Christ and the Father are exalted. This is the potential destiny of righteous man and woman. As the fulness of iniquity leads people to captivity by the adversary, so a fulness of truth leads to the total liberty of exaltation with the Father. This is what it means to grow "from grace to grace."

Abraham understood the relationship between righteousness and obedience to law and the reception of godly knowledge. Notice how the four following statements of Abraham show not only his desires, but the pattern we have been discussing.

"And, finding there was greater happiness and peace and rest for me, I sought for the blessings of the fathers . . . having been myself (1) a follower of righteousness, (2) desiring also to be one who possessed great knowledge, (3) and to be a greater follower of righteousness, (4) and to possess a greater knowledge." (Abraham 1:2)

Abraham adds another dimension to this pattern. He realized that "GREATER happiness and peace and rest" resulted from his desires for righteousness and knowledge. It is evident, therefore, that righteousness leads to knowledge, which leads to happiness and peace. This cycle then continues until one has not only a fulness of light and truth but also a fulness of joy.

The Light of Christ

Doctrine and Covenants 84 describes the starting point of progressing from one degree of light or grace to another while we are on this earth. The Lord explains the Light of Christ, introducing it by stating that "the word of the Lord is truth, and whatsoever is truth is light, and whatsoever is light is

Spirit, even the Spirit of Jesus Christ." That man might not be left without a sure guide in a fallen world, the Lord has provided that "the Spirit giveth light to every man that cometh into the world; and the Spirit enlighteneth every man through the world, that hearkeneth to the voice of the Spirit." Obedience is the key. "And every one that hearkeneth to the voice of the Spirit *cometh unto God,* even the Father." The Father then "teacheth him of the covenant," and progression from grace to grace follows. (D&C 84:45–48, italics added.)

Every individual has the Light of Christ. Obedience to that light leads one to the Father. Disobedience to that light, the scriptures teach, puts a person "under the bondage of sin" (D&C 84:49–51). These same truths, repeated in Doctrine and Covenants 93, help clarify the guidance of the Light of Christ. The Savior says: "Here is the agency of man, and here is the condemnation of man; because that which was from the beginning is plainly manifest unto them, and they receive not the light. And every man whose spirit receiveth not the light is under condemnation. For man is spirit." (D&C 93:31–33.)

All persons, as recipients of the Light of Christ, may exercise true agency in choosing to follow that which is "plainly manifest unto them." If they "receive not the light," they reject and fight an element that is deeply associated with them, "for man is spirit," the revelation explains. The spirit in man leads him to truth if he does not deaden its effect through disobedience. This last verse indicates that not only the Light of Christ but also man's own spirit directs him to truth and goodness.

"Intelligence Cleaveth unto Intelligence"

A very important truth relative to these principles is taught in Doctrine and Covenants 88:

> For intelligence cleaveth unto intelligence; wisdom receiveth wisdom; truth embraceth truth; virtue loveth virtue; light cleaveth unto light; mercy hath compassion on mercy and claimeth her own; justice continueth its course and

claimeth its own; judgment goeth before the face of him who sitteth upon the throne and governeth and executeth all things (D&C 88:40).

Like things attract one another. Intelligence, wisdom, truth, light, and mercy tend to gravitate toward each other. It is no surprise that the characteristics used in this verse correspond perfectly to the principles discussed earlier. Virtue, mercy, and justice are qualities of God's perfect character, just as are light, truth, and intelligence.

In practical terms, a person of intelligence, light, truth, and mercy will associate with and cleave to others who share the same characteristics. If the Light of Christ is given to every individual, and if "man is spirit," then it is natural for man to cleave to light, truth, and intelligence. Both the Light of Christ and his own spirit cause him to seek the Father, from whom he will learn "of the covenant."

It is easy to be confused or led astray when discussing these topics, because our knowledge is limited until further revelation is given concerning the Light of Christ, intelligence, and the spirit of man. An illustration may help clarify these principles. Many children have used a magnet to pull iron filings out of a sandbox. They can't see the filings in the sand, but as the magnet is pulled through the sand the dark filings cling to its surface. The basic elements of both the magnet and the iron filings are similar. They cleave to each other. Although this illustration is very simple, perhaps it can help us visualize the influence of Christ's light and the natural attraction of man's spirit to all that is good and true. There is light within all mankind which can pull intelligence and light from life and help the individual embrace God. The Light of Christ and man's own spirit act like magnets, cleaving to the truth and to those who teach it.

Each individual has a lesser or greater propensity to accept truth and righteousness. This may be explained in part by the premortal existence. Abraham learned that there were different degrees of intelligence among the multitudes of our

Father's spirit children. Some were "noble and great." Some studied and applied the great principles and truths of the gospel with greater eagerness and commitment. On earth, receiving light and truth is often like touching a memory. Jesus said, "My sheep hear my voice, and I know them, and they follow me" (John 10:27). It is natural we should do so; we followed his voice conscientiously in the premortal existence. We cleave to it on earth. We were strong spirits there and brought with us a certain propensity to cleave to the light. We grew from grace to grace there and continue to do so here. God has not left his children alone. Planted within us is an element that will, if obeyed, lead us to exaltation and eternal life.

9

THE NATURAL MAN

THERE IS SOMETHING THAT CAN BLOCK or hinder mankind from following the Light of Christ back to the Father. If that happens, man may not be taught "of the covenant." This hindrance is an integral part of man. It must be controlled, and eventually eliminated, or man will be led to the adversary and partake of his "fulness." This hindrance has several names in the scriptures, but most often it is called "the natural man" or "the flesh." This "natural man" resulted from the Fall.

Some associate the natural man too closely with the physical body of man and thus falsely condemn man's tabernacle. At the end of the Creation, God pronounced that "all things which I had made were very good" (Moses 2:31). Man was included in that pronouncement. The physical body of man is "good." Joseph Smith also taught that "the elements are eternal, and spirit and element, inseparably connected, receive a fulness of joy; and when separated, man cannot receive a fulness of joy" (D&C 93:33–34).

Once again, the concept of fulness is stressed. Since a "fulness of joy" cannot be achieved without the physical element, that physical element is not evil if controlled righteously. It is the carnal, untamed desires of the "flesh" that bring evil.

An Enemy to God

King Benjamin explained that "the natural man is an enemy to God, and has been from the fall of Adam, and will be, forever and ever" (Mosiah 3:19). However, if man "yields to

72

the enticings of the Holy Spirit," he will be able to "[put] off the natural man and [become] a saint through the atonement of Christ the Lord." Benjamin then gives the definition of a Saint as one who is "submissive, meek, humble, patient, full of love, willing to submit to all things which the Lord seeth fit to inflict upon him, even as a child doth submit to his father" (Mosiah 3:19). The natural man is called an "enemy" because man cannot become a Saint if he yields to the natural man. If the natural man is first "put off," the Holy Spirit can guide the individual. That Holy Spirit will cultivate in him the qualities of a Saint, making him meek, patient, full of love, and obedient.

If the natural man is not "put off," man then becomes, as expressed in Alma 42:10, "carnal, sensual, and devilish, by nature." The same verse refers to this life as a "preparatory state." The preparation needed is the death of the natural man. Those who remain in their natural, carnal, sensual, and devilish state may degenerate into the fulness of iniquity and suffer final captivity by the devil. There, in contrast to the Saint, one is required to "submit to all things" the devil "seeth fit to inflict upon him."

Alma also teaches that "all men that are in a state of *nature* . . . are in the gall of bitterness and . . . have gone contrary to the nature of God" (Alma 41:11, italics added). Abinadi speaks to the wicked priests of King Noah, warning them of their own "carnal and devilish" nature. He speaks of "the devil, . . . that old serpent that did beguile our first parents, which was the cause of their fall; which was the cause of all mankind becoming carnal, sensual, devilish, knowing evil from good, subjecting themselves to the devil. Thus all mankind were lost; and behold, they would have been endlessly lost were it not that God redeemed his people from their lost and fallen state." (Mosiah 16:3–4.) Abinadi then warns the wicked priests of the attitude that leads to the fulness of iniquity:

> Remember that he that persists in his own carnal nature, and goes on in the ways of sin and rebellion against God, remaineth in his fallen state and the devil hath all power over

him. Therefore he is as though there was no redemption made, being an enemy to God; and also is the devil an enemy to God. (Mosiah 16:5.)

Persists is an important word in the above quotation. It is not only the yielding to the natural man that creates a character like that of Lucifer; it is persistence in this path that is so damaging. The Fall brought the natural man, and, if followed persistently, the natural man leads to a carnal, sensual, and devilish character. It was this thought that caused Lehi to exhort Laman and Lemuel to choose righteousness and its resulting liberty, rather than evil with its resulting captivity. He pleaded with his sons to "not choose eternal death, according to the will of the flesh and the evil which is therein, which giveth the spirit of the devil power to captivate, to bring you down to hell, that he may reign over you in his own kingdom" (2 Nephi 2:29).

Honorable Men of the Earth

When one reads the Book of Mormon it appears that life is an either/or situation. Verses in the Bible also suggest that we are either for or against the Savior. We know through the revelations given to the Prophet Joseph Smith that there are three kingdoms of glory, and that in attaining the various glories of those kingdoms each individual is judged according to his or her life. Within the context of the natural man, as he is spoken of by the prophets in the Book of Mormon and the Bible, let us not forget the "honorable men of the earth" (D&C 76:75) who inherit terrestrial glory, not having accepted the fulness of the gospel but also not being consigned to telestial glory or outer darkness. We are also told by Joseph Smith that "there are many yet on the earth among all sects, parties, and denominations, who are blinded by the subtle craftiness of men, whereby they lie in wait to deceive, and who are only kept from the truth because they know not where to find it" (D&C 123:12).

The great work for the dead must be kept in mind lest we

become too narrow in our focus. "All who have died without a knowledge of this gospel, who would have received it if they had been permitted to tarry, shall be heirs of the celestial kingdom of God" (D&C 137:7). Yet there is wisdom in thinking of life as an either/or situation. In principle, most of the choices we make follow the enticings of the natural man or the light of God. It should not surprise us to find many different degrees of good and evil between the two major poles.

The Works of the Flesh

The Book of Mormon is not unique in its teachings about the natural man. The Pearl of Great Price teaches that some of Adam's children "loved Satan more than God. And men began from that time forth to be carnal, sensual, and devilish." (Moses 5:13.) The New Testament also identifies the natural man or "the flesh" as God's enemy, leading mankind to the adversary and the subsequent fulness of iniquity. Paul taught the Galatians much about the difference between following the inclinations of the flesh and following those of the Spirit. Notice how closely his teachings parallel those of King Benjamin:

> This I say then, Walk in the Spirit, and ye shall not fulfil the lust of the flesh.
>
> For the flesh lusteth against the Spirit, and the Spirit against the flesh: and these are contrary the one to the other: so that ye cannot do the things that ye would. . . .
>
> Now the works of the flesh are manifest, which are these; Adultery, fornication, uncleanness, lasciviousness,
>
> Idolatry, witchcraft, hatred, variance, emulations, wrath, strife, seditions, heresies,
>
> Envyings, murders, drunkenness, revellings, and such like: of the which I tell you before, as I have also told you in time past, that they which do such things shall not inherit the kingdom of God.
>
> But the fruit of the Spirit is love, joy, peace, long-suffering, gentleness, goodness, faith,

Meekness, temperance: against such there is no law.

And they that are Christ's have crucified the flesh with the affections and lusts.

If we live in the Spirit, let us also walk in the Spirit. (Galatians 5:16–17, 19–25.)

This is one of the plainest scriptures in the canon dealing with the contrasting characteristics of the natural man and those of the Spirit. In the Epistle to the Colossians, Paul adds to the list of qualities fostered by the natural man "inordinate affection, evil concupiscence, . . . covetousness, . . . anger, wrath, malice, blasphemy, filthy communication," and lying (Colossians 3:5–9). Man must choose to follow either the Light of Christ, which is given to every man, or the inclinations of the natural man, which is part of every man as a result of the Fall. One leads to adultery, lasciviousness, and murder, while the other encourages love, peace, and long-suffering.

"In Their Hearts"

Paul also taught the Ephesians about the flesh and its nature, with an important addition:

In time past ye walked according to the course of this world, according to the prince of the power of the air, the spirit that now worketh in the children of disobedience:

Among whom also we all had our conversation in times past in the lusts of our flesh, fulfilling the desires of the flesh and of the mind; and were by nature the children of wrath, even as others (Ephesians 2:2–3).

Paul taught that the natural man is not only manifested in the body, but may be found also in the mind. This is important to understand. It is closely associated with a teaching of the Pearl of Great Price in which the Lord explains to Adam that "inasmuch as thy children are conceived in sin, even so when they begin to grow up, *sin conceiveth in their hearts,* and they taste the bitter, that they may know to prize the good. And it is given unto them to know good from evil; wherefore they are agents unto themselves." (Moses 6:55–56; italics added.) The natural man is "in the heart." This critical phrase is understood more fully in light of the true meaning of being born again. In truth, the heart and mind are in all probability the real seat of the natural man. Do not the scriptures testify that "as [a man] thinketh in his heart, so is he" (Proverbs 23:7)?

The Natural Reaction

Insight into the natural man can be discovered through a few illustrations. Many men do not perceive the beginnings of a carnal, sensual, and devilish nature. If one reads in a novel or sees in a movie a suggestive scene, is not the *natural* reaction to dwell on it and feed the lust? If one person has more material possessions than another, is it not natural for one to feel proud and the other to feel envious? If a man injures another, is not the natural reaction to seek revenge? If someone swerves in front of you maliciously on the highway, is it not natural to get angry? Illustrations could be given of sloth, gluttony, man's pleasure at watching others fight, swearing, and other "natural" behaviors. Even Joseph Smith warned the men of the priesthood that it was "the nature and disposition of almost all men, as soon as they get a little authority, . . . to exercise unrighteous dominion" (D&C 121:39). These examples do not fit all individuals, but they should give us an idea of the natural man. One doesn't have to work to develop lust, selfishness, greed, pride, anger, envy, or violence. If uncontrolled they come naturally and grow in power and intensity of evil. They lead to the fulness of iniquity.

A World of Opposition

One may ask why the Fall was a desirable thing if it produced the natural man? Does not the gospel teach that the Fall was an integral part of the plan? Without the Fall there would have been no posterity for Adam and Eve; the Fall was necessary for people to obtain their physical bodies in order to have a "fulness of joy."

Not all answers have been given; however, we can obtain comfort from several thoughts concerning the natural man. First, through the Savior's atonement, the gift of the Holy Ghost, and spiritual rebirth we can overcome the natural man. This will be discussed in depth in the pages that follow. Second, this temporal, fallen world can help produce a character of godliness in spite of the evils that exist. Lehi taught that "it must needs be, that there is an opposition in all things. If not so, . . . righteousness could not be brought to pass." (2 Nephi 2:11.) The Fall brought about a world of opposition.

Righteousness is the choosing of good over evil. Without the opportunity for choice there can be no righteousness or happiness, for Lehi taught that "if there be no righteousness there be no happiness" (2 Nephi 2:13). Happiness results from choosing good when faced with evil, or from obeying when given the opportunity to disobey. Some will choose evil; they will obey the inclination of the natural man, and the sorrows, deaths, miseries, and sins the world has witnessed since its creation will result.

However, people rise to their greatest heights as sons and daughters of God when they try to minister to the needs of those who have harsh trials in life. Empathy is born from the ashes of suffering. Mercy comes from sorrow. Charity and service spring from the agonies of guilt and despair. Courage in its highest form is selfless and sacrificing. Awareness of the cruelties of man sharpens a sense of justice. To oppose evil makes one noble. Empathy, mercy, compassion, courage, justice, and selflessness are all qualities of godhood, qualities the Father wishes his children to cultivate. They are the characteristics that result in an individual's being worthy to receive light and truth. Man can allow the evils of the world to make him bitter and cynical, doubting the goodness of God; or he can let them make him Christlike, willing to sacrifice, through love, all that he is to fight the influences of those who give in to the natural man and become carnal, sensual, and devilish. Perhaps this is the best reply to the question, Why is there pain and suffering in the world?

Most parents would be willing to suffer great pain if they knew that their suffering would produce in their children the qualities of godhood. They would then know their children would grow in light and truth until they reached the state where all sorrow and pain are wiped away in the fulness of joy that accompanies exaltation.

With this perspective in mind, the necessity of the Fall becomes more apparent. Although the Fall brought with it the natural man, godliness can be achieved. Paul taught, "All things work together for good to them that love God" (Romans 8:28). Lehi taught, when speaking of the Fall, that "all things have been done in the wisdom of him who knoweth all things" (2 Nephi 2:24). The natural man can be controlled and eventually "put off." God has given men the tools necessary. All men have light and spirit. And though it is "natural" to seek evil, it is also natural to seek goodness. True progress is made when one is "born again," becoming a son or daughter of Christ. We will explore this process in the next chapter.

10

BORN AGAIN

BEING "BORN AGAIN" IS THE scriptural term for the process by which one "puts off the natural man" and becomes a Saint. The Christian world discusses at length the doctrine of being born again or "born of the Spirit." Much of this discussion leads believers to have faith in a salvation that comes by the simple acceptance of Christ as one's personal Savior without much effort on the part of the believer. A search through the scriptures, however, reveals that the process is more involved than this.

Being born again consists of both a death and a birth. It is a transition from one state of being to another, just as birth and death are. To be born again implies the death of the natural man, a figurative death that takes place in the heart. Remember, the Lord told Adam that when children "begin to grow up, sin conceiveth *in their hearts,* and they taste the bitter, that they may know to prize the good" (Moses 6:55; italics added). The Atonement plays a key role in changing a person's heart.

The Roots of Sin

After King Benjamin explained to his people the atonement of Christ, they were overcome by the Spirit. Although they were good people and had been "a diligent people in keeping the commandments of the Lord" (Mosiah 1:11), after hearing of the natural man and the Atonement they "viewed themselves in their own carnal state, even less than the dust of the earth."

They prayed for the cleansing mercy of the Atonement that they might "receive forgiveness of [their] sins, and [their] hearts may be purified." Their prayers were answered and they were "filled with joy, having received a remission of their sins, and having peace of conscience, because of the exceeding faith which they had in Jesus Christ." (Mosiah 4:2–3.)

Many truths emerge in these two verses. First, even a "diligent people" need to recognize "their own carnal state." This is not so much a recognition of specific sinful acts as of a sinfulness that results from the desires of one's heart. One begins to realize that the specific sin of snapping at a spouse or a child is really the result of impatience; "telling a neighbor off" is the result of pride or anger; adultery or fornication follows lust. One begins, through the Light of Christ, to see the roots of sin. As long as individuals concentrate on the outward acts and not on the heart, they will never be truly born again. As Lamoni's father prayed, so must all pray: "What shall I do that I may be born of God, having this wicked spirit rooted out of my breast, and receive his spirit?" (Alma 22:15.)

We learn another truth from Benjamin's people. When they recognize their sinfulness they ask that the atoning blood of Christ be applied in their behalf, that they might receive forgiveness and have their "hearts purified." They ask for this purification because of their faith in Christ. This is one of the finest examples in scripture of the practical results of having faith in the Savior's atonement. That faith leads one to seek the death of the natural man through purification of the heart. Faith in the Lord Jesus Christ is the only power whereby one may overcome the natural man.

Benjamin's people immediately receive the joy that comes with a remission of sins. It brings "peace of conscience." Mormon reminds his readers that this miracle was wrought because of the people's "exceeding faith . . . in Jesus Christ" (Mosiah 4:3). Being born again is one of the first steps on the road to receiving a fulness of light and truth, because it brings the purity of heart necessary to receive light and truth. It is also a step that must be taken before one gains the constant companionship of the Holy Ghost, who teaches light and truth and refines character.

The Mighty Change

At the end of his address Benjamin asks his people if they believe his words. Their reply is one of the best descriptions of the "born again" process in all scripture:

> And they all cried with one voice, saying: Yea, we believe all the words which thou hast spoken unto us; and also, we know of their surety and truth, because of the Spirit of the Lord Omnipotent, which has wrought a mighty change in us, or in our hearts, that we have no more disposition to do evil, but to do good continually (Mosiah 5:2).

A person who is born again has experienced this "mighty change" of heart. That person does not desire evil, but desires good. He is eager to listen to the voice of the Spirit, the Light of Christ, the prophets, and the scriptures, rather than to hold to the inclinations of the natural man. The person who has been born again may still be tempted to lust, greed, selfishness, and anger, but will seek to control those feelings and thoughts, continually bending his will to that of the Savior. This "mighty change" will be evidenced by a "broken heart and a contrite spirit," which betoken humility, not pride, in being "saved."

Whenever the Book of Mormon speaks of being born again, the heart is the center of the altered state. A few examples may help illustrate this truth. Speaking of the converted Lamanites, Alma tells us, "They did all declare unto the people the self-same thing—that their hearts had been changed; that they had no more desire to do evil" (Alma 19:33). The focus is on losing the desire for evil because of a change of heart through the atonement of Christ.

Alma the Younger speaks of these truths, which he learned by his own experience. He reminds the people of Zarahemla of his father's experience after listening to Abinadi: "There was a mighty change wrought in his heart." Alma continues, "He preached the word unto your fathers, and a mighty change was also wrought in their hearts, and they humbled themselves," and "they were faithful until the end; therefore they were saved." Alma then asks the crucial question: "And now behold, I ask of you, my brethren of the church, have ye spiritually been born of God? Have ye received his image in your countenances? Have ye experienced this mighty change in your hearts?" (Alma 5:11–14.)

The Image of Christ

Alma adds an important truth relative to the process of spiritual rebirth. The death of the natural man is but the beginning. We must then receive "[Christ's] image in [our] countenances." Remember, Benjamin's counsel was not only to put off the natural man; also a Saint has to be born. Saints have the image of Christ engraved on their countenance by a lifetime of righteousness. Alma reveals this truth the moment he awakens from his three-day sojourn in hell: "I have repented of my sins," he tells the people who prayed for his recovery, "and have been redeemed of the Lord; behold I am born of the Spirit." Alma testifies that his experience must be applied to all men:

> Marvel not that all mankind, yea, men and women, all nations, kindreds, tongues and people, must be born again; yea, born of God, changed from their carnal and fallen state, to a state of righteousness, being redeemed of God, becoming his sons and daughters;
> And thus they become new creatures; and unless they do this, they can in nowise inherit the kingdom of God. (Mosiah 27:24–26.)

Alma calls the spiritually reborn person a "new creature," a "son" or "daughter" of God. The "father" of this son or daughter is Jesus Christ. No father wants his child to remain forever a baby; progress, growth, and improvement in every worthy way are desired. Christ is a righteous, perfect father. He desires his children to "grow up" and be like him. They must follow his example and acquire all the traits and qualities he possesses, just as he followed the Father and attained his qualities and perfection by growing from grace to grace. The reborn son or daughter of Christ, having entered into a state of "grace" through the Atonement, then progresses from grace to grace until he or she has reached perfection. This progression is the fruit of having faith in Christ. This is the whole mission of mankind. One should seek to be as kind, gentle, meek, compassionate, merciful, and loving as Christ.

Paul teaches these truths plainly. In his epistles to the Galatians and the Colossians, Paul instructs the early Church members on the fruits of the Spirit. He contrasts these fruits with the fruits of the flesh, enumerated earlier. In describing the fruits of the Spirit he lists many of the qualities and characteristics of the Savior: "But the fruit of the Spirit is love, joy, peace, longsuffering, gentleness, goodness, faith, meekness, temperance: against such there is no law" (Galatians 5:22–23). In his Epistle to the Colossians he provides a similar list of qualities in contrast to those of the natural man. He reminds the Saints that they

> have put off the old man with his deeds;
> And have put on the new man, which is renewed in knowledge after the image of him that created him. . . .
> Put on therefore, as the elect of God, holy and beloved, bowels of mercies, kindness, humbleness of mind, meekness, longsuffering. . . .
> And above all these things put on charity, which is the bond of perfectness. (Colossians 3:9–10, 12, 14.)

The Reality of the Atonement

This creation of a "new creature" is dramatically portrayed in the life of Alma the Younger. Nowhere in scripture is the power of the Atonement seen in quite the same light. Before the Atonement "wrought a mighty change" in Alma, he was "a very wicked and an idolatrous man" (Mosiah 27:8). He used his power of speech to lead people away from God into all manner of iniquities. He caused "dissension" and gave "a chance for the enemy of God to exercise his power" over the people (Mosiah 27:9). He sought "to destroy the church of God" (Mosiah 27:10). He "rebelled" until an angel caused him to see his sinful life. While speaking of this experience in later years to his son Helaman, Alma describes the agonies of a damned soul:

> The very thought of coming into the presence of my God did rack my soul with inexpressible horror.
> Oh, thought I, that I could be banished and become extinct both soul and body, that I might not be brought to stand in the presence of my God, to be judged of my deeds. (Alma 36:14–15.)

He describes the pain and bitterness as he was "harrowed up to the greatest degree . . . with all [his] sins" (Alma 36:12). In the midst of this agony he cried within his heart, "O Jesus, thou Son of God, have mercy on me" (Alma 36:18). In the moment of that plea the Atonement took hold of Alma and he was born again. The mighty change took place. It was a change that had immediate and long-term effects:

> I could remember my pains no more; yea, I was harrowed up by the memory of my sins no more.
> And oh, what joy, and what marvelous light I did behold; yea, my soul was filled with joy as exceeding as was my pain!
> Yea, I say unto you, my son, that there could be nothing so exquisite and so bitter as were my pains. Yea, and again I say unto you, my son, that on the other hand, there can be nothing so exquisite and sweet as was my joy. (Alma 36:19–21.)

Before the mercy of the Atonement was extended, the

thought of coming before God filled Alma with horror. After the change Alma "saw . . . God sitting upon his throne, surrounded with numberless concourses of angels, in the attitude of singing and praising their God; yea, and [his] soul did long to be there" (Alma 36:22; italics added). Before this experience with the Savior, Alma fought the Church; afterwards he sought to build it up. Before, he was filled with wickedness and iniquity; after, his life was patterned according to the Savior's. Before, he rebelled; after, he submitted. In every aspect of his life Alma was a new creature. This shows the power of the Atonement and the result of being born again.

Though being born again affects individuals differently, they are all changed through their faith in Christ. They lose the desire to sin, wanting instead to become Christlike. This is what we mean when we say, "We believe that the first [principle] . . . of the Gospel [is] . . . Faith in the Lord Jesus Christ" (Articles of Faith 1:4). It is the first essential step on the pathway that leads to a fulness of light and truth.

In essence, all must choose which inclination they will follow. If we were to put together all we have discussed in the past two chapters, our understanding of progression towards a fulness of light and truth or the fulness of iniquity could be illustrated with the accompanying diagram.

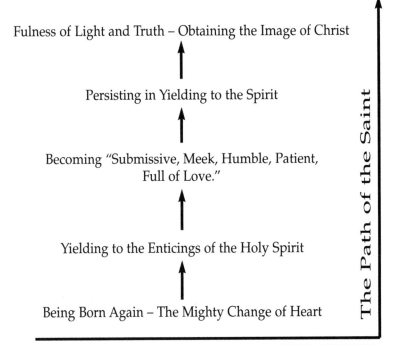

Fulness of Light and Truth – Obtaining the Image of Christ

↑

Persisting in Yielding to the Spirit

↑

Becoming "Submissive, Meek, Humble, Patient, Full of Love."

↑

Yielding to the Enticings of the Holy Spirit

↑

Being Born Again – The Mighty Change of Heart

The Path of the Saint

THE SPIRIT

THE FLESH

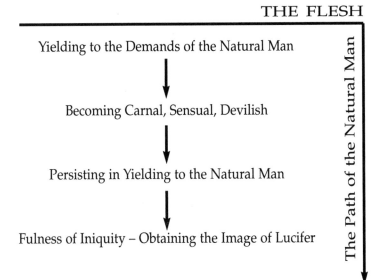

Yielding to the Demands of the Natural Man

↓

Becoming Carnal, Sensual, Devilish

↓

Persisting in Yielding to the Natural Man

↓

Fulness of Iniquity – Obtaining the Image of Lucifer

The Path of the Natural Man

11

FIRST PRINCIPLES AND LASTING EFFECT

THE ORDINANCE THAT SYMBOLIZES the rebirth and the mighty change of heart is baptism. It suggests to the mind both the death of the natural man and the birth of a saint, a son or daughter of Christ. The font represents the grave wherein the natural man is buried. The new child of Christ is resurrected from that burial. The font also represents the womb. As a child emerges from the water of his mother's womb, so too do we enter a new life from the waters of baptism. As a newborn child receives the name of his father, the newly baptized individual accepts the name of the father of his rebirth, that of Christ. Baptism symbolizes a cleansing from old sins. The new son or daughter is then clothed with the Holy Ghost.

Baptism—The Covenant of Rebirth

The new son or daughter of Christ now begins to mature, striving to become like his divine parent. Our baptismal covenants are essential in this growth process. In baptism certain covenants are made which, if honored, will naturally lead the new son or daughter of Christ to a fulness of light and truth. These covenants are repeated with each partaking of the sacrament. The sacrament symbolizes one's continual recommitment to the mighty change and the development of Christlike qualities through (1) taking upon oneself the name of Christ, (2) remembering him, and (3) keeping his commandments.

King Benjamin's people were "willing to enter into a covenant with . . . God to do his will, and to be *obedient to his commandments* in all things, . . . all the remainder of [their] days" (Mosiah 5:5, italics added). They were also willing to "be called the children of Christ, his sons, and his daughters," and to "take upon [themselves] the name of Christ." Benjamin exhorted them to "remember to retain the name written always in your hearts, that ye are not found on the left hand of God, but that ye hear and know the voice by which ye shall be called, and also, the name by which he shall call you. For how knoweth a man the master whom he has not served, and who is a stranger unto him, and is far from the thoughts and intents of his heart?" (Mosiah 5:7–8, 12–13.) Benjamin's people entered into all three sacramental covenants.

One keeps the commandments of God because they will lead him to a Christlike character. One remembers the Atonement because it will help him maintain the humility and broken heart necessary to retain a remission of sins. One also remembers the Savior because his life is the perfect example all must follow to become like the Father and win exaltation. A constant recommitment to take on oneself the name of Christ is a necessary reminder that one has covenanted to become like him, growing from grace to grace. Newborn sons and daughters of Christ promise to walk in their father's footsteps.

All these points are beautifully expressed in an experience of George Albert Smith:

A number of years ago I was seriously ill; in fact, I think everyone gave me up but my wife. . . . I became so weak as to be scarcely able to move. It was a slow and exhausting effort for me even to turn over in bed.

One day, under these conditions, I lost consciousness of my surroundings and thought I had passed to the other side. I found myself standing with my back to a large and beautiful lake, facing a great forest of trees. There was no one in sight, and there was no boat upon the lake or any other visible means to indicate how I might have arrived there. I realized, or seemed to realize, that I had finished my work in mortality and had gone home. I began to look around, to see if I could not find someone. There was no evidence of anyone living there, just those great, beautiful trees in front of me and the wonderful lake behind me.

I began to explore, and soon I found a trail through the woods which seemed to have been used very little, and which was almost obscured by grass. I followed this trail, and after I had walked for some time and had traveled a considerable distance through the forest, I saw a man coming towards me. I became aware that he was a very large man, and I hurried my steps to reach him, because I recognized him as my grandfather. . . . I remember how happy I was to see him coming. I had been given his name and had always been proud of it.

When Grandfather came within a few feet of me, he stopped. His stopping was an invitation for me to stop. Then . . . he looked at me very earnestly and said:

"I would like to know what you have done with my name."

Everything I had ever done passed before me as though it were a flying picture on a screen—everything I had done. Quickly this vivid retrospect came down to the very time I was standing there. My whole life had passed before me. I smiled and looked at my grandfather and said:

"I have never done anything with your name of which you need be ashamed."

He stepped forward and took me in his arms, and as he did so, I became conscious again of my earthly surroundings. My pillow was as wet as though water had been poured on it —wet with tears of gratitude that I could answer unashamed. (Leon R. Hartshorn, comp., *Classic Stories from the Lives of Our Prophets* [Salt Lake City: Deseret Book Co., 1971], pp. 238–39.)

All those who have been baptized have taken the name of Christ for their own. They should feel the same humility, reverence, and gratitude for that name that President Smith felt for his grandfather's name. Symbolically speaking, one day all true Christians will find themselves across the lake and walking down the path. They will see someone coming toward them, and the light of his countenance will pull them toward him, and they will long to embrace him. Perhaps he too will stop a few feet away and ask that all-important question: "What have you done with my name?" If one has experienced the mighty change and has kept his baptismal and sacramental covenants, he will look at the Savior and reply, "I have never done anything with your name of which you need be ashamed." Christ will then step forward and embrace his reborn son or daughter.

Many people have been given names of righteous men and women in the scriptures or of righteous ancestors. Often parents name their children after righteous persons in the hope and expectation that they will grow up to be like their namesake. In a simple manner this is part of the power behind taking the name of Christ. In baptism a person promises to "grow up" to be like the father of his or her rebirth—Jesus Christ.

Helaman gave his two sons the names of their "first parents," Lehi and Nephi, explaining to them that their names would serve as a constant reminder to act and live as did their ancestors. If we applied his reasoning to our bearing the name of Christ we could paraphrase Helaman's counsel in the following manner. Our Father in Heaven would say to us: "Behold, I have given unto you the name of [Christ] . . . and this I have done that when you remember your name ye may remember [him]; and when ye remember [him] ye may remember [his] works; and when ye remember [his] works ye may know how that it is said, and also written, that they were good. Therefore, my [children], I would that ye should do that which is good, that it may be said of you, and also written, even as it has been said and written of [him]." (Helaman 5:6–7.)

The Attitudes of Repentance

A lifetime of constant repentance is necessary if one is to report to the Savior that nothing has been done with his name worthy of condemnation. This is not the initial repentance inherent in the mighty change, when the desire to do evil is exchanged for the desire to do good. Rather it is the repentance one needs to continue a day-to-day progression. A Christlike character cannot be built in a single moment; it must be constantly nourished. Discouragement should not be the prevalent attitude, but hope. This is the gospel of hope. True sons and daughters of Christ are guided by the hope that perfection will come. They are not discouraged because perfection is still far distant, but they accept the fact that continual repentance and improvement are required. Alma asked the citizens of Zarahemla, "And now behold, I say unto you, my brethren, if ye have experienced a change of heart, and if ye have felt to sing the song of redeeming love, I would ask, can ye feel so now?" (Alma 5:26.)

Constant repentance helps one always feel like singing "the song of redeeming love." The steps of repentance are enumerated in many books and articles; however, the attitudes of repentance also need to be taught, for without these attitudes one will not proceed from grace to grace.

Saints have the desire to constantly improve their lives. As we discussed earlier, refining one's character brings further light and truth. However, the greater the light one has, the more readily one sees the need to improve. More light brings new commandments, instructions, and counsels. Obedience to this new light and truth refines the character and produces godliness. This in turn brings more light. Attitudes and behaviors not previously considered to be offensive to God are corrected as the son or daughter of Christ grows in the truth. This positive, upward climb is directed by hope, not despair.

Another attitude of repentance is often ignored. God does not want excuses for sins and disobedience; the Atonement was bought at too dear a price. Yet often people ask the Lord to excuse their sins rather than seek true repentance and forgiveness. Some rationalize their problems in terms of extenuating circumstances, trying to explain why they disobeyed instead of simply confessing their sin. It is often very difficult to say to the Lord, "I have broken thy commandments. I knew what I was doing and *there is no excuse for my behavior, my thoughts, or my words.* I ask for forgiveness." This requires true humility. There is pride in the individual who cannot say, "There is no excuse for my actions." Alma offered no excuse when he explained to his son Helaman how he felt before the Atonement cleansed him: "I saw that I had rebelled against my God, and that I had not kept his holy commandments. Yea, and I had murdered many of his children, or rather led them away unto destruction." (Alma 36:13–14.)

An "excuse my sins" attitude often leads to asking God to ignore the sin, not forgive it. In essence the sinner says to God, "Let me off the hook this time." The focus is on the removal of punishment. True repentance seeks to restore an endangered relationship. Sin grieves the Spirit of the Lord. The Spirit withdraws, or as Benjamin warned, "Ye do withdraw yourselves from the Spirit of the Lord" (Mosiah 2:36). God seeks a oneness with his children, a unity of mind and heart. True repentance does not ask to be "let off the hook," but exhibits genuine sorrow that sinful actions, thoughts, or words have placed a valued relationship in jeopardy. This attitude is beautifully expressed by David in the fifty-first Psalm: "Cast me not away from thy presence; and take not thy holy spirit from me. Restore unto me the joy of thy salvation; and uphold me with thy free spirit. . . . The sacrifices of God are a broken spirit: a broken and a contrite heart, O God, thou wilt not despise." (Psalm 51:11–12, 17.)

Christ called his disciples his friends. Sin threatens that friendship, a oneness dear enough to the Savior that he was willing to lay down his life for it. Those who receive his sacrifice must also cherish the oneness. When one who sins values the friendship, repentance comes with true humility, and character constantly improves. The individual is willing to accept counsel and do what is necessary to restore the precious relationship with the Lord and his Church.

The attitudes of repentance promote a continual purifying of the heart, which brings the light and truth necessary for the ultimate oneness promised by the Father and the Son. Benjamin promised one could "always retain a remission of your sins." Thus a person could "grow in the knowledge of the glory of him that created you, or in the knowledge of that which is just and true" (Mosiah 4:12).

The Gift of the Holy Ghost

The last ordinance spoken of in the fourth article of faith is the gift of the Holy Ghost. It is necessary to understand the first three principles and ordinances in order to realize what is required before an individual can receive the Holy Ghost. The statement in the ordinance of confirmation, "Receive the Holy Ghost," is more an invitation than a command or an automatic bestowal. The fact that we desire and are able to receive the light of the Spirit confirms our repentance and baptism. We truly are clean, for those whose deeds continue to be evil avoid the light of the Holy Ghost. Jesus taught this truth to Nicodemus, who came to him in the darkness. "For every one that doeth evil hateth the light, neither cometh to the light, lest his deeds should be reproved. But he that doeth truth cometh to the light, that his deeds may be made manifest, that they are wrought in God." (John 3:20–21.)

Becoming Christlike is a great challenge that we should pursue with hope. For this reason an individual receives the gift of the Holy Ghost after being baptized. The Holy Ghost is intended as a constant companion to help each recipient keep the baptismal covenants, grow in faith, and retain through continual repentance and humility a remission of sins. Remembering the relationship of light and truth to character and righteousness, we can see that the Holy Ghost is essential for reaching a fulness. The Holy Ghost does two basic things for those who accept his guidance. The Holy Ghost seeks to (1) purify and refine character by teaching the qualities of godliness, and (2) reveals increasing light and revelation, thereby helping the individual discern "the truth of all things" (Moroni 10:5).

Notice how completely the Savior's teachings about the Holy Ghost to his Apostles at the Last Supper dovetail with these two principles. Christ taught that "the Comforter, which is the Holy Ghost, whom the Father will send in my name, . . . shall teach you all things, and bring all things to your remembrance, whatsoever I have said unto you" (John 14:26). He called the Comforter "the Spirit of truth, which proceedeth from the Father," and he promised, "he shall testify of me" (John 15:26). The Holy Ghost would "reprove the world of sin, and of righteousness, and of judgment." Christ told the Apostles, "I have yet many things to say unto you, but ye cannot bear them now." Those truths would be revealed by the Holy Ghost, for he would "guide [them] into all truth . . . and shew [them] things to come." Christ explained the extent of knowledge that the Holy Ghost could bestow: "All things that the Father hath are mine: therefore said I, that he shall take of mine, and shall shew it unto you." (John 16:8, 12–13, 15.)

A summary of these teachings reveals that the Holy Ghost teaches, testifies, and brings to remembrance truth. He reproves sin and encourages righteousness and judgment. The "comfort" he brings is the peace that comes through obedience and a sure understanding of the principles of life and salvation contained in the gospel. Through proper application of given truth, all things can be revealed.

An analogy of a magnet was used earlier. This comparison can also be applied to the Holy Ghost. He is a being of light and truth. He knows all things. The Savior called him "the Spirit of truth" (John 16:13). Since intelligence cleaves to intelligence, light embraces light, and truth seeks truth, the Holy Ghost greatly enhances an individual's ability to receive and discern truth. Just as the magnet pulls from the sand the tiny iron filings, the Holy Ghost separates truth from error in the ideas, philosophies, teachings, and actions of men. Saints are not deceived; with the gift of the Holy Ghost they discern light and truth more easily. Joseph Smith discovered this immediately after his baptism: "We were filled with the Holy Ghost, and rejoiced in the God of our salvation," he wrote. "Our minds being now enlightened, we began to have the scriptures laid open to our understandings, and the true meaning and intention of their more mysterious passages revealed unto us in a manner which we never could attain to previously, nor ever before had thought of." (Joseph Smith—History 1:73–74.) This is not a unique experience. The scriptures are filled with examples of men who received great understanding through the power of the Holy Ghost. Each righteous member of the Church can testify of the revelatory power of the Holy Ghost.

The phrase "filled with the Holy Ghost" is significant. It is repeated often in the scriptures. We need not only the Holy Ghost's influence, but also to be "filled" with the Holy Ghost. This leaves no room for other spirits or attitudes that would lead on a downward path. Being filled with the Holy Ghost leads to being full of light and truth, as are the Father and the Son.

Also, as a magnet is able to order or organize the iron filings according to magnetic poles, the Holy Ghost can order, assimilate, interrelate, and compare truths until all truth is seen as unified and whole.

The promise of guidance from the Lord through the Holy Ghost is inherent in that all-encompassing promise in the sacrament prayer: "they may always have his Spirit to be with them" (D&C 20:77). When Nephi completed his teachings about the pathway to eternal life, he spoke of the power of the Holy Ghost. After describing the gate of faith, repentance, and baptism, Nephi promised his people that they would receive the Holy Ghost, and then added, "It will show unto you all things what ye should do" (2 Nephi 32:5).

Enduring to the End

The Holy Ghost leads a person to accomplish the last great challenge of the gospel—that of "enduring to the end." How does one endure, and to what end? Nephi speaks of these principles in his last great address. He gives perhaps the best definition of endurance in scripture:

And now, my beloved brethren, I know . . . that unless a man shall endure to the end, in following the example of the Son of the living God, he cannot be saved.

Wherefore, do the things which I have told you I have seen that your Lord and your Redeemer should do; for, for this cause have they been shown unto me, that ye might know the gate by which ye should enter. For the gate by which ye should enter is repentance and baptism by water; and then cometh a remission of your sins by fire and by the Holy Ghost.

And then are ye in this strait and narrow path which leads to eternal life; yea, ye have entered in by the gate; ye have done according to the commandments of the Father and the Son; and ye have received the Holy Ghost, which witnesses of the Father and the Son, unto the fulfilling of the promise which he hath made, that if ye entered in by the way ye should receive. (2 Nephi 31:16–18.)

Endurance means following "the example of the Son." In 2 Nephi 31 Nephi exhorts mankind to follow Christ's example of obedience five separate times (see verses 10, 12–13, 16–17). If a person spends his lifetime following Christ, he will acquire the attributes of godliness until he is like Christ and full of "grace and truth," as the Savior is full of grace and truth. Nephi follows this reiteration of the basic principles of the gospel by asking if "all is done." His answer is negative. As if to stress the meaning of endurance, Nephi gives a fuller definition of following the Son. You "must press forward with a steadfastness in Christ," he testifies, "having a perfect brightness of hope, and a love of God and of all men. Wherefore, if ye shall press forward, feasting upon the word of Christ, and endure to the end, behold, thus saith the Father: Ye shall have eternal life. And now, behold, my beloved brethren, this is the way." (2 Nephi 31:19–21.)

Endurance is not merely achieving a certain degree of righteousness and then leveling off, maintaining that degree until death. Endurance is progress, a steadfast pressing forward, feasting on all the words of Christ, which Nephi explains are given through the Holy Ghost:

And now, behold, my beloved brethren, I suppose that ye ponder somewhat in your hearts concerning that which ye should do after ye have entered in by the way. But, behold, why do ye ponder these things in your hearts? . . .

For behold, again I say unto you that if ye will enter in by the way, and receive the Holy Ghost, it will show unto you all things what ye should do.

Behold, this is the doctrine of Christ. (2 Nephi 32:1, 5–6.)

The "end" to which man must endure is not just the end of life. Rather, the end to which one progresses is godhood. To obtain it, the child of God must enter the gate of faith, repentance, baptism, and the gift of the Holy Ghost. This places him or her on the pathway. The pathway is a steady climb toward the perfection of Christ. At the "end" of the pathway is exaltation. Enduring to that end means following the Son of God fully.

We have not addressed the first principle of the gospel, that of faith, in detail, but the foundation for all the previous principles and ordinances is faith in the Savior. This faith rests on the knowledge of his character. King Benjamin emphasized numerous times that it was the "goodness" of the Lord that inspired the rebirth of his people. (See Mosiah 4:5,6,11.) One does not need to hesitate to go to the Savior for forgiveness. The Savior delights in granting it and "great is his joy in the soul that repenteth!" (D&C 18:13.) Faith is founded not only in an all-powerful being but also in the attributes and characteristics of that being. He is merciful, patient, long-suffering, compassionate, and so forth.

The Doctrine of Christ

The doctrine of Christ is simple and plain. One need not be a great scholar of the scriptures to understand it; it was never intended to be difficult or mysterious. The fulness of light and truth that brings exaltation comes from having faith in Christ, which leads to being born again and experiencing a mighty change of heart. That change kills the natural man and brings into existence a newborn son or daughter of Christ, symbolized by baptism. Through constant faith and repentance, and through keeping the baptismal and sacrament covenants, one is worthy of the companionship of the Holy Ghost. He, as a being of light and truth, refines, purifies, and sanctifies individuals, teaching them truth, showing them "all things" necessary for exaltation. Thus they grow from grace to grace. Thus they endure to the end in obedience to every principle, law, commandment, and counsel of God.

It is not a matter of doing all we can and then the Savior will do the rest, as is sometimes suggested. Instead it is a constant upward effort to reach the fulness of light and truth. We need not be discouraged, however, or lose hope. The Lord assures us he will not forsake us as long as we continue to strive. He cannot be satisfied with anything less than a character like his own, nor do we truly desire him to, but he will work with us until his Father can say of us as he said of him. "This is my Beloved Son." Through these simple principles gods are developed as individuals walk a pathway that is opposite to the one leading to a fulness of iniquity.

12

A ZION SOCIETY

AS WE HAVE SEEN, REJECTION of prophetic teachings contributes to the fulness of iniquity. In contrast, the acceptance of prophetic counsel guides one from grace to grace. It is from the scriptures, the prophets, and the Holy Ghost that light, truth, and intelligence are revealed. From these same sources, the principles and examples of righteous living are revealed. Therefore, giving heed to the prophets, especially the living ones, is of the utmost importance in enabling one to grow to a fulness in light and truth. To acquire a full confidence in the Lord's anointed servants, one needs to understand the close relationship the prophets have to the principles already discussed.

The Character of a Prophet

Prophets are worthy of man's confidence because of their righteousness, godliness, and character. If light, truth, and intelligence are contingent upon obedience and godliness, this should tell mankind something about the character of the men whom God has deemed worthy to receive and reveal his truths. A man such as Joseph Smith, who gave to the world so many revelations, had to have the character that receives such truth. Mormon taught that the Lord spoke to those "of strong faith and a firm mind in every form of godliness" (Moroni 7:30). This is not to say that prophets are perfect, but they do have the attributes of godliness in sufficient measure to hold and teach the revealed light of the Lord. Alma plainly taught this principle to the citizens of Ammonihah while speaking of

the chosen high priests who would "teach [God's] commandments unto the children of men, that they also might enter into
his rest" (Alma 13:6). Those high priests were

> called and prepared from the foundation of the world accord-
> ing to the foreknowledge of God, on account of their exceed-
> ing faith and good works; in the first place being left to choose
> good or evil; therefore they having chosen good, and exercis-
> ing exceedingly great faith, are called with a holy calling
> (Alma 13:3).

Prophets are called and prepared because of their "exceeding faith and good works." They have chosen good. They have
not rejected the Spirit of God. The abundance of light and truth
they give their fellowmen is evidence of their being approved
before God. Good works and faith precede their calls here on
the earth, as Abraham taught. He saw "the intelligences that
were organized before the world was; and among all these
there were many of the noble and great ones." Abraham saw
that these spirits "were good." God revealed to Abraham that
these noble spirits would be God's "rulers." Abraham was
"one of them." He was "chosen before [he was] born." (Abraham 3:22–23.)

To Govern and to Give Light

The Lord taught Abraham that there were different degrees
of intelligence among all his children. He compared the different intelligence levels among his spirit children to the different
degrees of light, magnitude, and rotational or orbital times
among the stars and planets of the universe. As there are "governing" stars in the heavens, so there would be governing
intelligences among men. As these governing stars of greater
magnitude "were set to give light" and life to the planets and
orbs close to them, so would the greater intelligences give
light and life to those who surrounded them. Just as the sun
"governs" the earth by keeping it in a controlled, true orbit in

space by its gravitational pull, so would the "noble and great" intelligences lead their people and keep them on a true course through life. This very powerful comparison gives dignity and nobility to the role of prophets (see Abraham 3).

The Lord's comparison continues. A single great star, Kolob, governs and gives light to the great governing stars. In the realm of God's children this great governing intelligence is Christ. He is "nearest" the throne of God. His role is to give light and order to all God's children. The "noble and great" prophets receive governing and light from him. Confidence can be given to prophets' counsels because of the assurance that Christ directs and teaches them so that they might govern and teach mankind.

Abraham's revelation also dealt with the test of earth life. He saw the Savior explain to the noble and great spirits that a world would be created where "we will prove them [the Father's children] herewith, to see if they will do all things whatsoever the Lord their God shall command them" (Abraham 3:25). Obedience is required; it is the focus of one's test on the earth. It seems a basic truth that an individual of intelligence should be able to recognize another being who has greater intelligence. It is imperative that those with less intelligence, light, and truth recognize the noble and great ones who possess light and truth more fully. With this recognition one is ready to be instructed and governed. Progress can proceed. However, if those with lesser intelligence cannot recognize the noble and great ones, thinking they are wiser themselves, they hinder their progression to a fulness of light and truth.

Because intelligence cleaves to intelligence, and truth to truth, the Light of Christ in every man and the influence of the Holy Ghost in those who have received this precious gift will cause the righteous to cleave to and embrace the teachings of the prophets. Following the prophets will lead to a fulness just as certainly as following the individual promptings of the Holy Ghost will. In our examination of the seven fulness-of-iniquity societies we have seen the destination of those who reject the prophets' words.

Through the darkness after the destruction of the wicked Nephites, the Savior's voice was heard. He specifically stated the reason some were destroyed while others were spared. "And it was the more righteous part of the people who were saved, and it was they who received the prophets and stoned them not; and it was they who had not shed the blood of the saints, who were spared." (3 Nephi 9:13; 10:12.)

During his subsequent visit with the "more righteous," the Savior, himself, taught that an essential key to the reception of the Holy Spirit and to being purified was the heed and faith given to the words of the prophets and apostles. Notice the words of his prayer while he was among the Nephites. "Father, I pray thee thou wilt give the Holy Ghost unto all them that shall believe in their [the Apostles] words. . . . Father, I thank thee that thou hast purified those whom I have chosen, [the Apostles] because of their faith, and I pray for them, and also for them who shall believe on their words, that they may be purified in me, through faith on their words, even as they are purified in me." (3 Nephi 19:21, 28.)

A Zion Society

With the foregoing principles in mind, we can understand a Zion society. Zion stands in opposition to the Babylon society of the world. As Babylon embodies all that is corrupt and decadent in the fulness of iniquity, Zion embodies all the beauty and joy that a fulness of light and truth can foster. All true prophets seek to establish Zion, and all truly reborn people try to live its principles. Through the guidance of the prophets and the endurance of the people, Zion is glorified in light and truth.

We know little about those people who have been successful in building a Zion society. Enoch's city accomplished it, as did Melchizedek's, and so did the Nephites after the visit of the Savior. It is prophesied that Zion will be built again and will flourish during the Millennium. The Doctrine and Covenants contains many instructions relative to the building up of Zion in the last days. Indeed, it can be described as a blueprint for Zion. Past Zion societies can reveal the basic characteristics of Zion just as the fulness-of-iniquity societies reveal those of Babylon.

Doctrine and Covenants 97 gives an excellent description of a Zion people: "Let Zion rejoice, for this is Zion—THE PURE IN HEART" (D&C 97:21). It is easy to see how completely this definition corresponds to the definition of a spiritually reborn person—the "mighty change" takes place in the heart, and purity of heart can be achieved. Purity was also promised to those who believed the words of the prophets.

The heart is also a focus of the description of Zion as it was built by Enoch's people: "And the Lord called his people ZION, because they were of one heart and one mind, and dwelt in righteousness; and there was no poor among them" (Moses 7:18). Four qualifications of Zion are evident in this verse. Its members are unified in heart and mind. Purity of heart leads to this "oneness" and fosters righteous living.

All Things Common

Oneness of mind and heart leads to a oneness of material blessings. There are no poor in a Zion society, because "every man esteem[s] his brother as himself" (D&C 38:24–25). This economic equality is common in all accounts of a Zion society. The Book of Mormon Nephites and Lamanites "had *all things common* among them; therefore there were not rich and poor, bond and free, but they were all made free, and partakers of the heavenly gift. . . . They were in one, the children of Christ." (4 Nephi 1:3, 17; italics added.) Sad to say, the abandonment of "all things common" was one of the leading causes that started the Nephite society on its downward spiral toward the fulness of iniquity. (See 4 Nephi 1:24–26.)

The early Saints of Jerusalem also practiced this economic concern, as stated in Acts 2:44. The law of Zion that brings about this condition is called the law of consecration. It is in direct contrast to the materialistic "power and gain" of a fulness-of-iniquity society. The Doctrine and Covenants gives a detailed explanation of its principles and practical applications. While a full examination of consecration is not within the scope of this work, some insight may be useful by way of contrast with the covetousness and greed of an alternative society. A few basic attitudes must exist for people to live this higher law. Notice how completely opposite they are to the laws of worldliness.

1. People must realize that God is the sole owner of the earth with all its resources: "I, the Lord, stretched out the heavens, and built the earth, my very handiwork; and all things therein are mine" (D&C 104:14).

2. If the earth belongs to the Lord, then mankind is a "steward" over God's possessions. He holds them in trust, to be used to further God's work on the earth. All that a man has belongs to God, including time, talents, and material blessings. "It is expedient that I, the Lord, should make every man accountable, as a steward over earthly blessings" (D&C 104:13).

3. There is no need for competitive accumulation of the earth's wealth and resources; God has declared that "*the earth is full,* and *there is enough* and to spare; yea, I prepared all things, and have given unto the children of men to be agents unto themselves" (D&C 104:17; italics added). It is ironic that the basic economic law of supply and demand is reversed in the Lord's wisdom. There is more supply than demand. In today's society, great lengths are often used to maintain just the opposite.

4. Charity and concern for fellowmen cause the wealthy in a Zion society to "impart of their substance." The Lord declared: "It is my purpose to provide for my saints, for all things are mine. But it must needs be done in mine own way; and behold this is the way that I, the Lord, have decreed to provide for my saints, that the poor shall be exalted, in that the rich are made low." (D&C 104:15–16.) Jacob encouraged the wealthy of his generation: "Think of your brethren like unto yourselves, and be familiar with all and free with your sub-

stance, that they may be rich like unto you" (Jacob 2:17). This attitude was encouraged among the saints of Missouri. The Lord described that he desired "every man seeking the interest of his neighbor, and doing all things with an eye single to the glory of God" (D&C 82:19).

5. Those in a Zion society labor to build up the kingdom of God and to care for the poor, and not for money, personal aggrandizement, or comfort: "The laborer in Zion shall labor for Zion; for if they labor for money they shall perish" (2 Nephi 26:31). If a Zion people are seeking wealth at all it is "for the intent to do good—to clothe the naked, and to feed the hungry, and to liberate the captive, and administer relief to the sick and the afflicted" (Jacob 2:19).

This last attitude causes those seeking Zion to "be anxiously engaged in a good cause, and do many things of their own free will, and bring to pass much righteousness; for the power is in them, wherein they are agents unto themselves. And inasmuch as men do good they shall in nowise lose their reward." (D&C 58:27–28.) This verse so beautifully characterizes Zion. They are willing to do everything the Lord asks them to do and more. There are numerous examples in the Doctrine and Covenants where the Lord gives counsel or expresses his will without commanding. These moments tested the attitudes of the Saints and allowed them to demonstrate to the Lord that they were worthy to begin the building process of Zion. (See D&C 63:22; 89:2–3.)

A prime attitude emerges in a Zion society—selflessness and charity. This is in direct opposition to the selfishness rampant in the iniquitous society. Remember, for the Nephites Zion ended when pride and prosperity caused them to break into classes, seeking "the fine things of the world" (4 Nephi 1:24) instead of "the welfare of Zion."

Beauty, Holiness, Cleanliness, Peace

Zion is described as a place of beauty and holiness: "For Zion must increase in beauty, and in holiness; her borders must be enlarged; her stakes must be strengthened; yea, verily I say unto you, Zion must arise and put on her beautiful garments" (D&C 82:14). This corresponds to the city of Enoch, which was also called "the City of Holiness" (Moses 7:19).

Purity, beauty, and holiness are contingent upon cleanliness. A cleanliness of both outer and inner resources is required. Zion is a place where virtue garnishes the thoughts unceasingly (D&C 121:45), rather than every man's thoughts were "only evil continually" (Moses 8:22). Purity of thought and feeling is difficult to achieve. Therefore, the Lord explains to his latter-day people that he will chasten Zion "until she overcomes and is clean before me" (D&C 90:36). He is a wise and a patient Lord, however—the chastening will be tempered with his mercy.

One of the blessings of Zion is the security it provides. Enoch's city "[dwelt] in safety" (Moses 7:20). Righteousness, safety, and prosperity all make Zion a stronghold of peace. Peace and lack of contention are mentioned six times in the first verses of 4 Nephi. That peace was the result of the people's being filled with the love of God. Mormon explained that "there was no contention in the land, because of the love of God which did dwell in the hearts of the people" (4 Nephi 1:15). The latter-day Zion is also spoken of as "a land of peace, a city of refuge, a place of safety" (D&C 45:66). Melchizedek's city was a place of "peace" and "righteousness," hence he was called "the prince of peace." (JST, Genesis 14:33–34; Alma 13:18.)

Happiness and Joy

All these conditions promote a feeling of happiness among the people. In truth, happiness comes in no other way. In describing the Nephites, Mormon remarked, "And surely there could not be a happier people among all the people who had been created by the hand of God" (4 Nephi 1:16).

We should ponder this trait of happiness in a Zion people.

"Men are, that they might have joy," the Book of Mormon teaches (2 Nephi 2:25). Joy and happiness are the aims of all people, but men are confused about how to obtain them. The Book of Mormon is plain. The first pages teach that the fruit of the tree of life produces the greatest happiness and joy. This fruit is above all things the most desirable, the most precious. However, people continue to seek happiness in the towers of the spacious building. That is why the building is described as symbolizing the "vain imaginations" of men (1 Nephi 12:18). Men vainly imagine that worldliness can produce joy. Alma proclaims that "wickedness never was happiness" (Alma 41:10). However, it is the verse immediately following this proclamation that holds so much meaning in light of the "natural man" and the contrasting "nature" of our Father in Heaven. Alma teaches:

> And now, my son, all men that are in a state of nature, or I would say, in a carnal state, are in the gall of bitterness and in the bonds of iniquity; they are without God in the world, and they have gone contrary to the nature of God; therefore, they are in a state contrary to the nature of happiness (Alma 41:11).

This powerful lesson is also taught by both Samuel the Lamanite and Mormon. Both speak to a people seeking happiness in the fulness of iniquity. From the walls of Zarahemla, Samuel foretells the words of an iniquitous people when the judgment comes. After describing their desire for the turning away of God's fulness of wrath, Samuel warns:

> Your days of probation are past; ye have procrastinated the day of your salvation until it is everlastingly too late, and your destruction is made sure; yea, for ye have sought all the days of your lives for that which ye could not obtain; and ye have sought for happiness in doing iniquity, which thing is contrary to the nature of that righteousness which is in our great and Eternal Head (Helaman 13:38).

Mormon had hoped that the sorrows of his fulness-of-iniquity people would bring repentance. He writes, "But behold this my joy was vain, for their sorrowing was not unto repentance, because of the goodness of God; but it was rather the sorrowing of the damned, because the Lord would not always suffer them to take happiness in sin" (Mormon 2:13).

Whenever one finds a people who experience true happiness, one finds a people striving for Zion and the fulness of light and truth. Lehi plainly teaches his sons that the only thing that produces happiness is righteousness. Happiness is by definition the pursuit of righteousness. "And if there be no righteousness there be no happiness. . . . And if these things are not there is no God." (2 Nephi 2:13.)

The Father desires his children to receive a "fulness of joy." The path to that "fulness" parallels the pathway of righteousness. Joy and happiness increase as one continues from grace to grace and is "glorified in truth and knoweth all things" (D&C 93:28).

This happiness can be achieved even while surrounded by a troubled world moving toward a fulness of iniquity. Zion's creation and maintenance does not hinge on outside forces. Mormon, commenting on a period of war among the Nephites, engraved this insightful addition: "And those who were faithful in keeping the commandments of the Lord were delivered at all times whilst thousands of their wicked brethren have been consigned to bondage, or to perish by the sword, or to dwindle in unbelief, and mingle with the Lamanites. But behold there never was a happier time among the people of Nephi, since the days of Nephi, than in the days of Moroni." (Alma 50:22–23.) In Mormon's mind it was critical that future generations understood that happiness can flourish in times of uncertainty and war, if there is personal righteousness. Evil does not have the power to blackmail joy.

Two Main Attitudes of Zion

One last description of Zion will serve as a capstone to the happiness, peace, holiness, safety, and purity that Zion represents. This description explains the two attitudes that drive forward all who seek Zion. Zion is a place where (1) "every man seek[s] the interest of his neighbor, and (2) do[es] all things with an eye single to the glory of God" (D&C 82:19). It is easy to see in this verse the two great commandments of the gospel as they are explained in both the Old and the New Testament. In these books men are commanded to "love the Lord thy God with all thy heart, and with all thy soul, and with all thy strength, and with all thy mind; and thy neighbor as thyself" (Luke 10:27). Seeking the interest of one's neighbor and focusing all attention and desires on the glory of God qualify one for the building up of Zion. We should remember that having an eye single to the glory of God is also crucial for receiving light and truth.

All Prophets Seek Zion

The end to which all prophets seek to lead their people is Zion. A true prophet will always try to achieve Zion through personal righteousness and integrity. Other types of leaders, politicians, and revolutionaries will promise the peace, unity, security, economic equality, and happiness of Zion, but will not seek to secure those blessings through consecration, purity, righteousness, selflessness, and obedience to eternal law; rather they will seek to establish it through revolution, force, deception, or legislation. This century has seen many attempts to create the blessings of Zion, from the Russian Revolution in the early decades to the "great society" of the sixties. Men have written and spoken of utopias, new deals, wars on poverty, new world orders, and nations where equality of race, gender, and class dominate the lives of their citizens. Often the catch phrases that name these movements sound hauntingly familiar to Zion. Obviously, the desire for a Zion society lies deep in humanity's heart. But these efforts, though sometimes well-intended, usually end with poor or dissipated results, if not total failure. This is one of the great tests of a true prophet. Joseph Smith taught these truths as he contemplated the city of

Enoch. It was revealed to him that "holy men" of all times sought for Zion through righteousness:

> Wherefore, hearken ye together and let me show unto you even my wisdom—the wisdom of him whom ye say is the God of Enoch, and his brethren,
> Who were separated from the earth, and were received unto myself—a city reserved until a day of righteousness shall come—a day which was sought for by all holy men, and they found it not because of wickedness and abominations;
> And confessed they were strangers and pilgrims on the earth;
> But obtained a promise that they should find it and see it in their flesh. (D&C 45:11–14.)

Joseph Smith did endeavor to bring his people to the happiness Zion provides. He did not succeed in his lifetime. Nor did Moses, but he strived for the same end.

> Moses . . . sought diligently to sanctify his people that they might behold the face of God;
> But they hardened their hearts and could not endure his presence; therefore, the Lord in his wrath, for his anger was kindled against them, swore that they should not enter into his rest while in the wilderness, which rest is the fulness of his glory. (D&C 84:23–24.)

Other prophets besides Enoch succeeded in building Zion; one of those prophets was Melchizedek. The Joseph Smith Translation of Genesis 14 reveals that Melchizedek's people "wrought righteousness, and obtained heaven, and sought for the city of Enoch which God had before taken, separating it from the earth, having reserved it unto the latter days, or the end of the world" (verse 34). How did Melchizedek accomplish this? He "did preach repentance unto his people. And behold, they did repent; and Melchizedek did establish peace in the land in his days." (Alma 13:18.) However, Melchizedek started with a people who "had waxed strong in iniquity and abomination; yea, they had all gone astray; they were full of all manner of wickedness" (Alma 13:17). Evidently his people were on the road to the fulness that leads to destruction. If the preaching of the gospel could turn Melchizedek's society around, we have great reason to hope for our own, for we too have men like Melchizedek leading the Church and boldly speaking out to the world. The 1995 Proclamation on The Family is an example of their message.

The rejection of prophets like Melchizedek leads to the fulness of iniquity inherent in Babylon; so, in like manner, does the acceptance of such prophets lead to the fulness of joy and light found only in Zion. True prophets, the fulness of light and truth, and a Zion society are inseparably connected. In spite of the obvious downward direction of our own nation, we have reason to hope in the noble and great ones of the day.

The Sons and Daughters of Christ Seek Zion

To what end will a spiritually reborn people progress when they endure through constant faith in Christ, repentance, obedience to covenants and prophets, and heeding of the directing light of the Holy Ghost? Perhaps nowhere in scripture is a Zion society so closely related to truly born-again people than in King Benjamin's address.

After his people experience the mighty change of heart through their faith in the Atonement, Benjamin teaches them what will follow if they remain true. Notice how closely the traits Benjamin enumerates resemble the definitions of a Zion people given in scripture. Benjamin exhorts his people to do four things: (1) "remember, and always retain in remembrance, the greatness of God"; (2) "humble yourselves even in the depths of humility"; (3) "[call] on the name of the Lord daily"; and (4) "[stand] steadfastly in the faith of that which is to come" (Mosiah 4:11). Benjamin then promises: "If ye do this ye shall always rejoice, and be filled with the love of God, and always retain a remission of your sins; and ye shall grow in the knowledge of the glory of him that created you, or in the knowledge of that which is just and true. And ye will not have a mind to injure one another, but to live peaceably, and to render to every man according to that which is his due. And . . . ye will teach [your children] to walk in the ways of truth and soberness; ye will teach them to love one another, and to serve one another. And also, ye yourselves will succor those that stand in need of your succor; ye will administer of your substance unto him that standeth in need." (Mosiah 4:12–16.)

These promises correspond perfectly to a Zion society. A son or daughter of Christ will build Zion as a natural result of his or her conversion. If we need more evidence that the death of the "natural man" and the creation of a "son or daughter of Christ" leads to Zion, the example of the Anti-Nephi-Lehies supplies it. These people also experienced the change of heart and lost the desire to sin. So great was their abhorrence of sin and their love for their fellowmen that "they buried their weapons . . . of war, for peace" (Alma 24:19). They were a happy and a righteous people who grew from day to day in their knowledge of God. They were "distinguished for their zeal towards God, and also towards men; for they were perfectly honest and upright in all things; and they were firm in the faith of Christ, even unto the end" (Alma 27:27).

Some in the Church dream about living during the Millennium and long for that day. There is nothing wrong with this desire, but the examples of Melchizedek's and Benjamin's people and the Anti-Nephi-Lehies show that one need not wait for the Millennium to enjoy a Zion society. It can be established in one's home, in the wards and stakes of Zion, indeed throughout the Church. In Benjamin's words, this condition can exist among people who have experienced the mighty change, who remember the greatness of God, humble themselves, call on the name of the Lord daily, and stand steadfastly in the faith of Christ. If a people *endure* in these things, Zion will be their end. This requires constant improvement. But over the years the results will be glorious. Latter-day Saints can follow the example of the early Nephites:

They did fast and pray oft, and did wax stronger and stronger in their humility, and firmer and firmer in the faith of Christ, unto the filling their souls with joy and consolation, yea, even to the purifying and the sanctification of their hearts, which sanctification cometh because of their yielding their hearts unto God (Helaman 3:35).

One Heart and One Mind

The prophets promise one final "end" to those who endure in living the principles of a Zion society. It is spoken of in the context of Zion, but its full meaning is perhaps not always comprehended. It was stressed time and time again by the Savior. He suffered the Atonement to prepare the way for it. It is wonderful to think that moments before entering the Garden of Gethsemane to begin the atoning sacrifice, Jesus prayed for the end to which he desired all men to endure: total oneness with each other and with the Godhead.

In his great Intercessory Prayer recorded in John 17, Christ prayed for all his disciples. Notice how many of the major themes we have discussed are unified in the words of the Master:

> And now I am no more in the world, but these are in the world. . . . I kept them in thy name: those that thou gavest me I have kept, and none of them is lost, but the son of perdition; that the scripture might be fulfilled. . . .
>
> I pray not that thou shouldest take them out of the world, but that thou shouldest keep them from the evil.
>
> They are not of the world, even as I am not of the world.
>
> Sanctify them through thy truth: thy word is truth.
>
> As thou hast sent me into the world, even so have I also sent them into the world.
>
> And for their sakes I sanctify myself, that they also might be sanctified through the truth.
>
> Neither pray I for these alone, but for them also which shall believe on me through their word;
>
> That they all may be one; as thou, Father, art in me, and I

in thee, that they also may be one in us: that the world may believe that thou hast sent me.

And the glory which thou gavest me I have given them; that they may be one, even as we are one:

I in them, and thou in me, that they may be made perfect in one; and that the world may know that thou hast sent me, and hast loved them, as thou hast loved me. (John 17:11–12, 15–23.)

Zion is described as a society where people are "of one heart and one mind" (Moses 7:18). This must be true of people's relationships with one another, for at the Last Supper Jesus taught his disciples to love each other. He indicates that if they are not one, they are not his disciples. He tells them that all the world will know they are his disciples by this oneness. John the Beloved stresses these same truths very eloquently in his First Epistle.

The Zion society presents a great contrast to the fulness of iniquity society. Babylon is a society of hate, war, greed, pride, and contention. It is the spirit manifested by the anti-Christ, for it represents everything foreign to the Master. Unity, oneness, and love are the identifying principles of true disciples. Those who foster contention, violence, war, and hatred are anti-Christs, because they oppose the harmony Christ sought to establish. In 4 Nephi the Zion people are described as not having "any manner of -ites; but they were in one, the children of Christ, and heirs to the kingdom of God" (4 Nephi 1:17).

To be sons and daughters of Christ implies achieving this oneness with his other disciples. But it also implies oneness with the Father, the Son, and the Holy Ghost. Christ prayed for that oneness. Zion is "of one heart and one mind" with the Father also, and this oneness is directly related to a fulness of joy and a fulness of light and truth. Light, truth, intelligence, virtue, mercy, justice, and wisdom, we are told, cleave to, embrace, receive, love, and claim their own. Two beings who are filled with these qualities will be one in the deepest meaning of the word. Therefore, the end to which God desires his children to endure is this total oneness. Then each child will cleave to, embrace, receive, and love the Father, the Son, and the Holy Ghost. To this end all things pertaining to the gospel of Jesus Christ will lead man. In that oneness, the fulness of light, truth, joy, and exaltation is found.

Man will then be "worthy of a far more, and an exceeding, and an eternal weight of glory" (D&C 132:16). But that "weight" must be won through the plan established by the Father, carried out by his Son, testified of by the Holy Ghost, and taught by his holy prophets. One of the highest ordinances that brings this "weight of glory" comes in the holy temples of the Lord. In these sacred edifices a husband and wife, children and parents, are sealed to each other in "the new and everlasting covenant." They become "one" for all eternity. That covenant, we are told, "was instituted for the fulness of my glory; and he that receiveth a fulness thereof must and shall abide the law, or he shall be damned, saith the Lord God" (D&C 132:6). The sealing power of temple ordinances ensures for the obedient seeker of truth the fulness of God's glory for all eternity. In this manner "is the continuation of the works of my Father, wherein he glorifieth himself" (D&C 132:31).

In the closing chapters of the Book of Mormon, Mormon summarizes the major truths of the gospel by showing their relationship to each other:

> The first fruits of repentance is baptism; and baptism cometh by faith unto the fulfilling the commandments; and the fulfilling the commandments bringeth remission of sins;
>
> And the remission of sins bringeth meekness, and lowliness of heart; and because of meekness and lowliness of heart cometh the visitation of the Holy Ghost, which Comforter filleth with hope and perfect love, which love endureth by diligence unto prayer, until the end shall come, when all the saints shall dwell with God. (Moroni 8:25–26.)

A Zion society reaches a point where it is so righteous that the Lord takes it from the earth, eventually to dwell in his presence for eternity, to enjoy the fulness of light and truth. A Babylon society reaches a point through the fulness of iniquity when the Lord removes it from the earth, to be cut off from his presence, because the people would not heed his counsels. The choice belongs to each of us. Will we feed at the tree of life, or will we make forbidden fruits our constant diet? Before we choose we must comprehend the fulness to which each road leads—the fulness of iniquity or the fulness of light and truth.

INDEX